# WASHINGTON, D.C. IN YOUR POCKET

**A handy directory of restaurants, hotels, museums, theaters, stores, nightlife, famous landmarks—the best of the city's sights, services, and pleasures!**

**Fourth Edition**

**BARRON'S**

Woodbury, New York • London • Toronto
Sydney

# Credits

Washington metro map reprinted courtesy of Metropolitan Area Transit Authority.

Book design by Milton Glaser, Inc.
Illustrations by Marc Rosenthal

Inclusion of a particular store or service in this guide should not be construed as a recommendation from the Publisher. All noted sources and services subject to change; we suggest that you phone ahead.

All inquiries should be addressed to:
Barron's Educational Series, Inc.
113 Crossways Park Drive
Woodbury, New York 11797

Library of Congress Catalog Card No. 86-22364

International Standard Book No. 0-8120-3757-X

Library of Congress Cataloging in
Publication Data

Washington, D.C. in your pocket

  Bibliography: p. 32
  1. Washington (D.C.)—Description—1981—
—Guide-books   I. Barron's Educational Series, Inc.
F192.3.W324   1987      917.53'044  86-22364
ISBN 0-8120-3757-X

PRINTED IN THE UNITED STATES OF AMERICA

789   969   987654321

# CONTENTS

Contents

Contents

Contents

vi

# PREFACE

Washington welcomes you! Possibly there is no other city in the world that has more museums, galleries, and cultural events open to the public without charge. This is the nation's capital, and that means most of these museums and sights are yours to enjoy.

Washington, D.C., is where the federal government does its work, whether it be from the White House, Congress, or Department of Agriculture. You can tour the workings of government: see how the FBI catches its most-wanted criminals; observe the Supreme Court make decisions that change the course of history; listen to your representatives in Congress fight for your interests.

Washington is stereotyped as a town of endless bureaucracy as well as high-powered politics, yet in recent years this sophisticated city has diversified enough to become a cultural center for the nation as well. The John F. Kennedy Center premieres plays and offers outstanding concerts. The museums display their valuable collections and also feature special exhibits. The greatest achievements of the American people are noted here, from the exhibits of technological progress in the Smithsonian Institution to the striking monuments of the country's past leaders. This is a city that reflects a large and diverse country, and you will find elements here from all its regions.

Washington, D.C., is an exciting city, with much to see and do. Enjoy its nightlife. Sample its ethnic restaurants. Whether you are here for business or pleasure, you'll find that Washington will exhilarate and challenge you. This is a directory to that Washington, not only covering the sights and sounds but also the businesses that make it move. It includes listings of hotels and restaurants, as any guide will, but also shops that offer unusual gifts, services such as day care, spots to eat the best ice cream or chocolate, places to go ice skating or bicycling, and tips to finding out about current music, theater, dancing, or just relaxing. We have taken the best of the city and listed it in this little directory, small enough to fit into your pocket or purse.

# Acknowledgments

We gratefully acknowledge the help of Helen Dole Griffith in researching and writing the material for this book.

# FINDING YOUR WAY AROUND TOWN

The city's layout, best observed from such promontories as the Washington Monument or the National Cathedral's Pilgrim Observation Tower, echoes the grid plans and grand boulevards of European cities. Visitors navigating Washington will quickly appreciate the efficiencies inherent in Pierre L'Enfant's plan. Although born in France (1754), L'Enfant—U.S. engineer, architect, and soldier—became devoted to the cause of Americans. In a 1789 letter to George Washington, he pointed out the unique opportunity for a nation to plan its capital without hindrances. (The area was formerly Maryland farmland with its share of creeks and swamps.)

L'Enfant's plan for Washington included a large share of circles. (Remember that those already on the circle have the right of way.) He divided the city into quadrants: Northwest (N.W.) with the majority of addresses; Southwest; Northeast; and Southeast. The major dividing lines intersect at the U.S. Capitol: East Capitol Street joins the Mall and runs east-west; North Capitol Street joins South Capitol Street and runs north-south. Streets are identified by the quadrant in which they are located (N.W., S.W., N.E., S.E.).

Odd-numbered addresses are on your right when you stand with your back to East Capitol or North Capitol or South Capitol Streets or the Mall. Streets running east-west are designated alphabetically. Streets running north-south are designated numerically. Streets running diagonally and major thoroughfares are named for states.

This system enables you to pinpoint fairly well your location. For example, if the address is the Esplanade Mall at 1990 K Street, N.W., the entrance is on K Street between 19th and 20th Streets (along the east side of 20th Street actually). Or suppose the address is the Connecticut Connection shopping mall at 1101 Connecticut Avenue, N.W.: To find the cross street, first count to the 11th letter of the alphabet.

(*Note*: Normally, this would be K. However, rumor has it that Pierre L'Enfant did not care for John Jay, first chief justice of the United States—1789–1795—so he eliminated the J in naming streets; the 11th letter of the alphabet then becomes L.) Sure enough, Connecticut Connection is at L Street. (There are no X, Y, or Z streets, either.)

Soon you will comprehend all of this. When the alphabet runs out, the streets have 2-syllable names, then 3-syllable names, then names of trees and flowers all the way to the Maryland line. L'Enfant lived his later years in relative obscurity, for his plan for Washington with its broad tree-lined streets was not implemented until after his death (1825). His gravesite in Arlington National Cemetery overlooks the city he conceived.

# AFTERNOON TEA

**Garden Terrace** At the Four Seasons Hotel, 2800 Pennsylvania Avenue, N.W.; 342-0444. A real English high tea is served from 3 to 4:30 PM weekdays and 3 to 5 PM weekends. Quite pleasant, sun-filled room.
**Radisson Henley Park** 926 Massachusetts Avenue, N.W. (Gallery Place or Metro Center Metro stops); 638-5200. English high tea is served in the Wilkes Room daily 4–6 PM. Scones and light sandwiches, and of course a variety of teas to choose from.
**Suzanne's Cafe** At the Phillips Collection, 1600 21st Street, N.W. (Dupont Circle); 483-7779. Located on the lower level of this wonderful art museum is a cafe open Tuesday–Saturday, 10 AM–4:30 PM, and Sunday, 2–4:30 PM, serving light lunch, a variety of pastries, and tea with Irish soda bread and fresh raspberry jam. A special tea menu is available for groups upon request and with advance notice. In the afternoon, a light menu of cheese and pâté is served at the Suzanne's on Connecticut Avenue. (See RESTAURANTS.)

# AMUSEMENT PARKS

**Kings Dominion** Doswell, Va. 23047; 804/876-5000. 75 miles south of Washington. Entrance fee includes unlimited use of all rides, roller coasters (including the 2-minute "Shock Wave" stand-up roller coaster), Safari monorail, etc. Open weekends from late March to early April; open daily approximately Memorial Day through Labor Day. Front gate opens 9:30 AM; rides open at 10:30 AM. Closes 8 PM on Sundays and 10 PM on Saturdays in the spring; closes 10 PM daily July–late August.

**Wild World** 13710 Central Avenue, Mitchellville, Md. 20716; 301/249-1500. Family recreation park. Entrance fee includes water activities (including the largest wave pool in the world), shows, 2 separate children's parks, rides, and roller coaster. Open April through October, 10 AM to 10–11 PM. Hours and days open may vary during the off-season. Call for up-to-date schedule. From the Beltway, take Exit 15A or 17A to Route 214 East (Central Avenue) approximately 4 miles on the left. See signs.

# ANNUAL EVENTS

This is a very brief list of the festivals, concerts, and events in Washington. For more ideas refer to INFORMATION—CALENDAR OF EVENTS. Also read "Weekend," published Fridays in the *Washington Post*, and *Calendar of Events*, a quarterly brochure published for free distribution by the Washington Convention and Visitors Association (See INFORMATION). *Calendar of Events* is the most thorough list of activities published in advance of the spring, summer, fall, and winter seasons.

# January

**National Capital Auto Show** Early January at the Washington Convention Center (371-4200).

**Washington Antique Show & Sale** Shoreham Hotel, 2500 Calvert Street, N.W. Approximately mid-January. Lectures and dinner dance by reservation. Watch for ads in the *Washington Post*, or call the Shoreham, 234-0700, ext. 6777.

**Chinese New Year Parade** Celebrated in Chinatown. H Street N.W. between 5th and 9th Streets (842-0130).

**Martin Luther King, Jr.'s Birthday** Celebrated at the Martin Luther King, Jr. Library (901 G Street, N.W.) and throughout the city on January 15 or close to it (727-1186).

**Inauguration of the 42nd President of the United States** January 1989. Always the third Tuesday of January. Inaugural Address in the morning on the steps of the U.S. Capitol followed by the parade down Pennsylvania Avenue to the White House.

# February

**Black History Month** The Kennedy Center has a very popular children's festival. Request a brochure in January (254-3600). Special events in libraries, museums, and art galleries throughout Washington. For programs at the Martin Luther King, Jr. Library, call 727-1186. For programs at the Smithsonian, call 357-2700.

**Birthdays** George Washington's birthday is celebrated at Mount Vernon and at the Washington Monument on February 22, and Abraham Lincoln's birthday is celebrated on February 12 at the Lincoln Memorial (426-6975).

**Annual Brazilian Carnival** This popular event features a Brazilian orchestra for samba dancing and a costume parade with prizes for best costume. Held the Saturday before Ash Wednesday, 8 PM–2 AM. Sponsored by the District of Columbia Partners of Brasilia, Inc., P.O. Box 40737, Washington, D.C. 20016; 301/229-0104. Write or call for ticket information. Portion of the ticket is tax deductible. Carnival is usually held at the Shoreham Hotel.

**State of the Union Message** The President of the United States addresses both houses of Congress in mid-February. Telecast live over major networks.

**Annual Events**

# March

**Virginia Slims of Washington Tennis Championships**
George Washington University, Smith Center, 22nd
and G Streets, N.W. (Foggy Bottom Metro stop); 429-
0690. About the third week in March. Women's tennis.

**Imagination Celebration for Children at the
Kennedy Center** (see April for details).

**Flower and Garden Show** Two and one-half acres of
flowers and assorted greenery. Garden tools, lawn furniture, etc., for sale. D.C. Convention Center, 9th and
H Streets, N.W. (Metro Center Metro stop, H Street
exit and Gallery Place stop); 371-4200. Fee charged.

**Kite-Flying Contest** Sponsored by the Smithsonian on
the Washington Monument grounds, usually the last
Saturday in March. To enter the contest you must
have a kite made entirely by hand (357-3030).

**Cherry Blossom Festival** The Park Service sets the
date about 10 days in advance of the festival date determined by the maturity of the buds and weather conditions (426-6975 or 426-6690). The opening of the festival is at the Tidal Basin with a lantern-lighting
ceremony in the evening.

**Annual One-Act Play Tournament** Local amateur
theater groups compete in this multi-weekend event.
Sponsored by the D.C. Department of Recreation (673-
7660). Fee charged.

**St. Patrick's Day Parade** Always on the Sunday before
St. Patrick's Day from 1 to 3:30 PM. Begins at 7th
Street, N.W. along Constitution Avenue to 18th
Street. Bagpipers, marching bands, floats, and lots of
Irish cheer! (301/424-2200).

# April

**Cherry Blossom Festival** Might be in early April if not
in late March (see March listing for details). The Jay-
cees sponsors a parade of high school marching bands
from across the country the first or second Saturday
in April (April 11, 1987). Other gala events include a
fashion show and ball. (296-8675 or 293-0480).

**American College Theatre Festival** At the Terrace
Theatre, Kennedy Center. For further information
write Kennedy Center, ACTF, Washington, D.C.
20566 (254-3437). Free tickets are distributed on a
Saturday morning in late March.

**Spring at the White House** Tour the spring gardens (426-6975 or 456-7041).

**Annual Canal Trek Hike** 10 miles along the C&O Canal for the benefit of the National Kidney Foundation, 2233 Wisconsin Avenue, N.W., Suite 320, Washington, D.C. 20007; 337-6600. Kickoff begins at 8 AM at the Georgetown Park entrance to the Canal. Entry fee.

**Easter Egg Roll** On the White House grounds (always the first Monday after Easter Sunday) (426-6975). 10 AM to 2 PM. For children 8 years and under, who must be accompanied by an adult. Very popular.

**Thomas Jefferson's Birthday** Celebrated at the Jefferson Memorial with a traditional wreath-laying ceremony (426-6690).

**National Capital Open Bicycle Race** Mid-April. The starter race of the year with participants from across the country. On the Ellipse. HEY-BIKE (439-2453).

**Georgetown House Tour** For brochure, write St. Johns Church, Georgetown Parish, 3240 O Street, N.W., Washington, D.C. 20007; 338-1796. Tickets about $10.

**Cleveland Park House Tour** Includes 7 or 8 unusual and prominent homes in this area of town. The walking tour benefits the National Child Research Center and begins from their headquarters, 3209 Highland Place, N.W., Washington, D.C. 20008; 363-8777.

**Imagination Celebration** An annual festival for children, held at the Kennedy Center the week before and the week after Easter (254-3600).

**Georgetown Garden Tour** Dumbarton Oaks gardens often included. Sponsored by Georgetown Children's House, 3224 N Street, N.W., Washington, D.C. 20007; 333-4953. Tax-deductible tickets may be purchased in advance. Children under 12 free.

**Annual Gross National Parade** Celebrates silliness; usually held the Sunday following Easter, 2–4 PM. Participants have included the Synchronized Precision Briefcase Drill Team, the Tax Flashers, and the Right to Arm Bears. The route is from 18th and M Streets, N.W., to the heart of Georgetown, at Wisconsin and M Streets. Sponsored by WMAL Radio for the benefit of the D.C. Police Boys and Girls Club. Listen to WMAL (630 AM) or call them for further information (686-3100).

**Ringling Bros.-Barnum & Bailey Circus** At the D.C. Starplex Armory for 2 weeks (547-9077).

**William Shakespeare's Birthday** Celebrated in Elizabethan style at the Folger Shakespeare Library, 201 E. Capitol Street, S.E. Open house, birthday cake, exhibits, demonstrations, performances, and children's activities. Always on a Saturday, 10 AM–4 PM, around Shakespeare's birthday (April 23). Free. Call for exact date of celebration (544-7077).

**The Washington Craft Show** Late April or early May. Sponsored by the Women's Committee of the Smithsonian Associates. Departmental Auditorium, 1301 Constitution Avenue, N.W. (357-4000). Friday, Saturday, and Sunday. Tickets sold at door. (For 1987, the dates are April 24, 25, and 26.)

# May

**Marine Corps Band, Drum and Bugle Corps, and Silent Drill Platoon** Friday evening 2-hour performances early May through early September. See THINGS TO DO for details.

**Flower Mart** On the grounds of the Washington National Cathedral. Early May. Hot dogs and sandwiches, children's activities, and carousel (537-6200).

**Capitol Hill House and Garden Tour** Always held on Mother's Day, this tour includes 6 or 7 homes and gardens, a tea, and jitney service! Sponsored by the Capitol Hill Restoration Society, 1002 Pennsylvania Avenue, S.E., Washington, D.C. 20003; 543-0425. Tour begins at Eastern Market, 7th Street and North Carolina Avenue, S.E.

**Annual Friendship House Market Day** Always the first Sunday in May, weather permitting, this street fair attracts people of all ages and interests. Market Row at the Eastern Market is blocked off to become the midway for the fair, with vendors selling a delectable variety of international and ethnic foods and craftspeople selling their creations. Children's games too! Proceeds support services for low-income Washington residents; sponsored by Friendship House, 619 D Street, S.E., Washington, D.C. 20003; 675-9050. Use the Metro to the Eastern Market station because parking is limited.

**Tour of the Embassies** About 8 embassies on a tour

sponsored by the Goodwill Industries. First or second Saturday in May; 11 AM–5:30 PM. Tax-deductible, non-refundable ticket includes shuttle bus, tea, receiving line. Goodwill Public Relations office will give you name of person to contact or where to watch for advertisements (636-4225).

**Hometown Run and Festival** Benefitting the Washington Urban League, there is a 15-kilometer and a 3-kilometer run followed by a festival on Western Plaza (14th Street and Pennsylvania Avenue) featuring entertainment and food. For information and registration forms, contact Washington Urban League, 3501 14th Street, N.W., Washington, D.C. 20010; 265-8200.

**Memorial Day Celebration** Wreath-laying ceremony at the Tomb of the Unknown Soldier, Arlington National Cemetery (426-6975).

**The National Symphony Orchestra** Their first free outdoor concert of the season is from the west lawn of the Capitol, 8 PM (426-6975).

## June

**Dupont Kalorama Museum Walk Day** Festivities for all ages, the first Saturday in June (387-2151). Features exhibitions, tours, special family activities, and live entertainment from noon to 4 PM at museums and galleries, members of the Dupont Kalorama Museums Consortium. On this day, museums that otherwise charge admission are free. See MUSEUMS.

**Annual D.C. Chili Cook Off** Sponsored by the National Kidney Foundation, 2233 Wisconsin Avenue, N.W., Suite 320, Washington, D.C. 20007; 337-6600. Fee to participate in the cook off includes membership in the International Chili Society. A small donation allows you to enjoy the entertainment and get a taste of chili concoctions. Winner is awarded a free trip to Tropico, California, for the International Chili Championship in October.

**Wianki** A Polish celebration of Midsummer Night and St. John's Eve is celebrated at the Reflecting Pool, Lincoln Memorial steps. Usually held on a Friday or Saturday evening close to the summer solstice. Watch newspapers for exact date of the event (426-6975).

**Gay and Lesbian Pride Parade** Held mid-June on Father's Day. (See GAY SCENE—EVENTS for details.)

**Festival of American Folk Life** Last week of June and first week of July, 11 AM–7 PM (357-2700). Performances by traditional musicians, dancers, and singers and demonstrations by craftsmen from around the United States. On the Smithsonian grounds.

**Potomac Riverfest** Every weekend in June, noon to dark, along Water Street, S.W. (adjacent to Maine Avenue), celebrating the revitalization of Washington's Potomac River. The parade kicks off the festival, followed by an elaborate opening celebration. Entertainment of every description, including music, fun run, fishing clinic and tournament, and canoe races from Fletcher's Boat House on the C&O Canal. Fireworks displays. Children's specialties, and plenty of food, tall ships, 4 stages of entertainment. Family event. Ride the Metro to L'Enfant Plaza. For further information, call D.C. Department of Recreation, 673-7660.

**National Old Timers Baseball Classic** At RFK Stadium. The National League of Old Timers take on the host American League (546-3337).

**Inside/Out at the Kennedy Center** The Friends of the Kennedy Center sponsor this event, generally the third Sunday in June, from noon to 8 PM. Eighty performing groups, seminars, and workshops help introduce the Kennedy Center to the public. Suitable for families. Food sold outside the Center. Free. For further information, call 254-8700.

## July

**D.C. Loft Jazz Festival** Showcases Washington's jazz artists and international groups. Held for several days, culminating July 5. Free events outdoors in the vicinity of 7th and D Streets, N.W. Tickets sold for programs at dc space. Managed by District Curators, 783-0360, or call dc space, 347-4960.

**Festival of American Folk Life** Continues on the Smithsonian grounds. (See June for details.)

**July 4 Fireworks** On the Mall at the Washington Monument. Parade down Constitution Avenue at 10 AM. Free concert by the National Symphony Orchestra on the west lawn of the Capitol about 8 PM, which is also a great vantage point for the fireworks at 9:15 PM. Another place to view the fireworks is from the rooftop of the Kennedy Center. Free tickets are distributed at

the Kennedy Center, Hall of the States, the Sunday
before July 4 at 10 AM. Limit of 5 tickets per person.
Each person, including children, who wishes to watch
the fireworks from this vantage point must have a
ticket.

**Annual Hispanic-American Cultural Festival** Cultural,
educational, and entertainment activities representing 21 countries are celebrated throughout July, culminating in a gala dance, street festival, and parade
in the heart of the Adams Morgan neighborhood. Tra-
ditionally held the last weekend of July. Organized by
the Hispanic Festival Committee (232-2820).

**Bastille Day Waiter's Race** Sponsored by Dominique's
restaurant. Always on July 14 about noon. Watch
waiters from Washington's restaurants race with a
tray carrying a split of champagne from 20th Street
and Pennsylvania Avenue, N.W., down to the White
House and back to Dominique's. Very popular event
(452-1126).

**Sovran Bank/D.C. National Tennis Classic** Rock Creek
Tennis Stadium, 16th and Kennedy Streets, N.W.
Mid-July. (429-0690). This men's tennis event is on
the International Grand Prix circuit. Prudential/
Bache Securities Grand Champions also playing at the
same time.

**Volleyball Tournament on the Mall** A Saturday or
Sunday—maybe even a 2-day tournament! Sponsored
by and for the benefit of the National Kidney Foundation, 2233 Wisconsin Avenue, N.W., Suite 320,
Washington, D.C. 20007; 337-6600. Fee to participate
but not to cheer!

# August

**Annual Children's Concert** By the Navy Band, Jefferson Memorial. Mid-to-late August. 7:30 PM (433-
2394).

# September

**ADD Arts: A Washington Celebration** Focuses on 500
visual and performing artists the Sunday before Labor
Day. Three outdoor stages, films, exhibits, and art activities for all ages are arranged in the Gallery Place

Metro stop area, 9th and F Streets, N.W. Food, drink, and craft items for sale. Fun for families. Free. Noon 'til midnight. Managed by District Curators, 783-0360.

**Adams Morgan Day Festival** Highlights the unique ethnic neighborhood in ½ mile of space. Five hundred booths offering special foods, crafts, causes, and concerns are accompanied by musical, theatrical, and dance entertainment. Children's activities too. Always the first Sunday after Labor Day. For further information, call this number from June through September: 462-5113.

**Annual Croquet Tournament** On the Ellipse across from the Organization of American States. Usually held the 3rd or 4th weekend in September. Round-robin tournament; instruction available (234-4602).

**Washington National Cathedral Annual Open House** Late September or early October. Festivities for all ages, including antique carousel (537-6200).

## October

**Oktoberfest Celebrations** Popular in the restaurants and outdoors.

**Decorator Show House** On display for the entire month. Local interior designers decorate an entire house. Admission proceeds benefit the National Symphony Orchestra. Watch news media for further details.

**Columbus Day Ceremony** At the Columbus statue in front of Union Station, October 12 (426-6975).

**Greek Festival** Held at Saint Sophia's Greek Orthodox Cathedral, 36th Street and Massachusetts Avenue, N.W. This picnic welcomes fall with native foods, Greek folk dancing, music, and special games for children. Mid-October, Friday–Sunday (333-4730).

**National Jousting Tournament** In mid-October. South of the Lincoln Memorial from 9 AM to 6 PM (426-6975).

**Fall Garden Tour** White House Gardens (426-6975).

**United States Supreme Court Opens** Sessions are open to the public (252-3211).

**International Horse Show** At the Capital Centre (see STADIUMS AND SPORTS ARENAS), late October–early November. Well advertised.

# November

**Marine Corps Marathon** Always the first Sunday of November (433-2854). A 26-mile course past Washington's monuments.

**Veteran's Day Ceremonies** Arlington National Cemetery, Tomb of the Unknown Soldier (426-6975). Wreath-laying by the president or other high-ranking official. November 11.

**Christmas Bazaars** Abundant in Washington area's churches and embassies in late November and early December. Watch for announcements in "Weekend" on Fridays in the *Washington Post*.

# December

**Ford's Theater** A play suitable for families is presented during the holiday season, late November through December (347-4833).

**U.S. Air Force Band Concert** DAR Constitution Hall, early December. Tickets go quickly—inquire in early November (767-5658/4310).

**YWCA International Fair** One day in early December (or late November) at the Washington Hilton, 1919 Connecticut Avenue, N.W. (638-2100).

**Georgetown Greens Sale & Christmas Bazaar** St. John's Church, 3240 O Street, N.W., one Saturday early in December (338-1796).

**Pageant of Peace and Lighting of the National Christmas Tree** On the Ellipse between the White House and the Washington Monument on Constitution Avenue about 5 PM (Dial-a-Park, 426-6975).

**Christmas at the White House** Tour the winter gardens (426-6975). Candlelight tours of the White House in its holiday finery are given in late December (456-7041).

**Hanukkah and Christmas Celebrations at the Kennedy Center** Variety of musical and theatrical events for all ages, many free (254-3776).

**Hanukkah Festival at B'nai B'rith Klutznick Museum** Holiday music and food the Sunday before Hanukkah. (See MUSEUMS.) (857-6583).

**Washington Cathedral Christmas Pageant** December 24. Children's service, 4 PM; Christmas Eve service, 10 PM; Christmas Day service, 10 AM. (537-6200).

**New Year's Eve Celebration at the Old Post Office Pavilion** and throughout the city. Features free top-name entertainment, ballroom dancing, and special menus at Pavilion's restaurants. The "countdown to midnight" culminates in a giant stamp dropped from the Post Office's historic clock tower. Sponsored by the D.C. Department of Recreation (673-7660).

# ANTIQUES

## Shops

These are just a few of the many antique shops in Washington. The D.C. Yellow Pages has the best list under "Antiques." Shops are open Monday–Saturday about 9 to 5 and have restricted hours during the summer. Frequent antique shows are held at the Washington Convention Center (371-4200).

**Arpad Antiques, Inc.** 3222 O Street, N.W. (Georgetown); 337-3424. Silver, furniture.

**Gonzalez** 2313 Calvert Street, N.W. (Upper Connecticut Avenue); 234-3336. China, porcelain, paintings, furniture, silverware, glassware, art, glass, chandeliers. Chandelier repair. Also open Friday evenings.

**Peter Mack Brown** 1525 Wisconsin Avenue, N.W. (Georgetown); 338-8484. Eighteenth-century furniture and decorative arts.

**Susquehanna Antique Company** 1319 Wisconsin Avenue, N.W. (Georgetown); 333-5843 and 333-1511. Two floors of furniture, silver, porcelains, engravings, and accessories.

**Tiny Jewel Box** 1143 Connecticut Avenue, N.W.; 393-2747. Antique jewelry.

## Auctioneers and Appraisers

**Adam A. Weschler & Son** 905–909 E Street, N.W.; Washington, D.C. 20004 (downtown); 628-1281. Weekly auctions on Tuesday at 9:30 AM. Also periodic catalogue sales of fine antiques, etc. Free illustrated brochure on request. Appraisals.

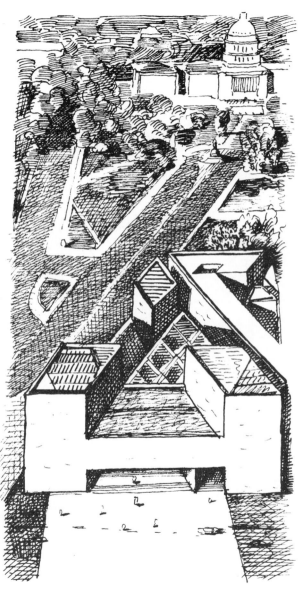

NEW EAST WING OF NATIONAL GALLERY

**C. G. Sloan & Company, Inc.** 919 E Street, N.W.: Washington, D.C. 20004; 628-1468. Frequent 3-day weekend catalogue sales of fine art, antiques, and collectibles. Free brochure on request. Sales advertised in classifieds. Office in Baltimore, 863 North Howard Street, Baltimore, Md. 21201; 301/669-5066. Also at 4950 Wyaconda Road, Rockville, Md. 20852; 301/468-4911. Appraisals of fine art and antiques.

**Sotheby's** 2903 M Street, N.W.; 298-8400. Consultations only; auction galleries in New York.

# ART GALLERIES

The following publications list current shows. "Weekend," published Fridays in the *Washington Post*; the *Washingtonian* magazine; and *Galleries*, a guide to Washington art galleries available in most galleries. *Museum Washington* is an excellent bimonthly publication (see NEWSPAPERS AND MAGAZINES).

Galleries are generally open Tuesday through Saturday, 11 AM–5 PM. Some are also open evenings and Sundays and by appointment. Many close all or part of August. Verification advised.

Galleries specializing in American crafts are listed under CRAFT SHOPS AND GALLERIES.

The **Washington Art Dealers Association, Inc., (WADA)**, a nonprofit organization incorporated in 1981, was established to provide a forum for discussion of issues and events of cultural interest in the city, to promote the interests of firms dealing in works of fine art, to improve the stature of the fine arts business, and to increase the public confidence toward responsible art dealers. Membership as of April 1986 is indicated.

**District Curators** While not a gallery, District Curators can steer you in the proper direction if you are looking for the work of a specific artist or for a gallery carrying a special style of art. Also, up-to-date on avant-garde performance arts. Their address is 930 F Street, N.W., Suite 700; 783-0360.

**Adams, Davidson Galleries** 3233 P Street, N.W. (Georgetown); 965-3800. Nineteenth-century and early 20th-century American paintings. Member, WADA.

**Addison-Ripley Gallery** 9 Hillyer Court (behind the Phillips Collection); 328-2332. Contemporary American art. Member, WADA.

**Anne Hathaway Gallery** Folger Library, 201 East Capitol Street; 547-2818. Contemporary paintings and ceramics.

**Anton Gallery** 2108 R Street, N.W. (Dupont Circle); 328-0823. Contemporary painting, sculpture, prints, and ceramics by local and regional artists. Member, WADA.

**Art Barn** 2401 Tilden Street, N.W. (uptown in Rock Creek Park); 426-6719. Nonprofit gallery showing works by Washington area artists and craftsmen. Closed Monday, Tuesday, and holidays. Tours and art classes for adults and children; reservations necessary. Also evening cultural arts programs in music, poetry, and art. Art demonstrations Sundays, 1–3 PM.

**Arts Club of Washington** 2017 I Street, N.W. (downtown); 331-7282. Contemporary American art.

**Atlantic Gallery** Foundry Building, 1055 Thomas Jefferson Street, N.W. (Georgetown); 337-2299. Nineteenth-century marine, sporting, and hunting scenes.

**Baumgartner Galleries** 2016 R Street, N.W. (Dupont Circle); 232-6320. Specializes in fine contemporary works by Washington, D.C., and Austrian artists. Member, WADA.

**B. R. Kornblatt Gallery** 406 7th Street, N.W. (downtown); 638-7657. Contemporary American art. Member, WADA.

**Capitol East Graphics** 600 E Street, S.E. (Capitol Hill, one block from Eastern Market Metro stop); 547-8246. Twentieth-century American and European printmakers, including better-known Afro-American artists. Nonrepresentational works on paper and sculpture.

**David Adamson Gallery** 406 7th Street, N.W. (downtown); 628-3862. Twentieth-century works on paper, and publishers of prints. Member, WADA.

**Fendrick Gallery** 3059 M Street, N.W. (Georgetown); 338-4544. The best in contemporary American art, including decorative art. Member, WADA.

**Fondo del Sol Visual Art & Media Center** 2112 R Street, N.W. (Dupont Circle); 483-2777. Alternative gallery showing art including photography and video by Hispanic, native American, and Afro-American artists. Free video shows every Saturday afternoon. Wednesday–Saturday 12:30–5 PM. Member, Dupont Circle Kalorama Museums Consortium (see MUSEUMS).

**Foundry Gallery** 404 7th Street, N.W. (downtown); 783-2757. Contemporary art, including decorative art by Washington artists.

**Franz Bader Gallery & Bookstore** 1701 Pennsylvania Avenue, N.W. (downtown); 659-5515. Concurrent sculpture and painting exhibitions; contemporary art by D.C. artists; Canadian Eskimo art; large selection of original international graphics. Also largest selection of art books in Washington.

**Gallery 10** 1519 Connecticut Avenue, N.W.; 232-3326. Contemporary art mainly by East Coast artists.

**Gallery K** 2010 R Street, N.W. (Dupont Circle); 223-6955. Contemporary. Member, WADA.

**Govinda Gallery** 1227 34th Street, N.W. (Georgetown); 333-1180. Broad selection of paintings, drawings, prints, silkscreens, and photography by a variety of local and well-known contemporary artists, as well as 19th- and early 20th-century shows from time to time. Member, WADA.

**Henri Gallery** 1500 21st Street, N.W. (Dupont Circle); 659-9313. Avant-garde.

**Hom Gallery** 2103 O Street, N.W. (Dupont Circle); 466-4076. Old masters and early 20th-century American and European masters. Member, WADA and Art Dealers Association of America.

**Jane Haslem Gallery** 406 7th Street, N.W. (downtown); 638-6162. American art from 1900 to the present. Member, WADA.

**Kathleen Ewing Gallery** 1609 Connecticut Avenue, N.W., Suite 200; 328-0955. Nineteenth-century, early 20th-century, and contemporary fine art photography. Member, WADA.

**Lansburgh's Cultural Center** 420 7th Street, N.W. (downtown); 724-2180. Galleries and studios for Washington artists.

**Local 1734 Art Collective** 1734 Connecticut Avenue, N.W. (Dupont Circle); 797-9264. Mixed media by local artists, with broad selection of silkscreen prints. Classes available.

**McIntosh/Drysdale Gallery** 406 7th Street, N.W. (downtown); 783-5190. Contemporary American and European art: sculpture, paintings, drawings, and photographs. Member, WADA.

**Martin Gallery** 2427 18th Street, N.W. (Adams Morgan); 232-1995. Nineteenth- and 20th-century photography with emphasis on contemporary photography; some works on paper.

**Mickelson Gallery** 707 G Street, N.W. (downtown); 628-1735. Prints, sculpture, and paintings. Fine museum framing. Member, WADA.

**Middendorf Gallery** 2009 Columbia Road, N.W. (Adams Morgan); 462-2009. Twentieth-century American art. Member, WADA.

**Old Print Gallery** 1220 31st Street, N.W. (Georgetown); 965-1818. Eighteenth- and 19th-century American prints and maps.

**(The) Olshonsky** 443 7th Street, N.W. (downtown); 737-5177. Washington artists.

**Osuna Gallery** 406 7th Street, N.W. (downtown); 296-1963. Paintings, drawings, and sculpture by contemporary American and Latin American artists. Also, Old Master paintings at 1914 16th Street, N.W., by appointment only. Member, WADA.

**Shogun Gallery** 1083 Wisconsin Avenue, N.W. (Georgetown); 965-5454. Three centuries of Japanese woodblock prints.

**Slavin Gallery** 404 7th Street, N.W. (downtown); 347-0473. Contemporary Washington artists and sculptors.

**Spectrum** 1132 29th Street, N.W. (Georgetown); 333-0954. Nonprofit local artists' cooperative.

**Taggart, Jorgensen & Putnam** 3241 P Street, N.W. (Georgetown); 298-7676. Nineteenth- and early 20th-century American painting and British watercolors. Member, WADA.

**Tolley Galleries** 821 15th Street, N.W. Suite 100 (downtown); 347-0003. Nineteenth- , early-20th century, and contemporary art. Portraits on commission.

**Touchstone Gallery** 2130 P Street, N.W. (Dupont Circle); 223-6683. Cooperative gallery showing paintings and sculpture by local artists.

**Trocadero** 1501 Connecticut Avenue, N.W. (Dupont Circle); 234-5656. Far Eastern art including bronzes, porcelain, and stone sculpture.

**Art**

**Veerhoff Galleries** 1512 Connecticut Avenue, N.W. (Dupont Circle); 387-2322. Since 1871. Contemporary American realists. Framing.

**Venable-Neslage-Rosen Galleries** 1803 Connecticut Avenue, N.W.; 462-1800. Paintings, sculpture, and original prints by contemporary American and European artists.

**Volta Place Gallery** 1531 33rd Street, N.W. at Volta Place (Georgetown); 342-2003. African art including fine ceremonial masks and statues, beadwork, jewelry, and fabric. Member, WADA.

**Washington Printmakers' Gallery** 1832 Jefferson Place, N.W. (Dupont Circle); 463-8847. Nonprofit gallery showing members' works, as well as art of visiting printmakers.

**Washington Project for the Arts (WPA)** 404 7th Street, N.W. (downtown); 347-8304. Local artists. WPA also has a bookstore and theater at 400 7th Street. Vibrant, enthusiastic shows.

**Watergate Gallery, Ltd.** Watergate Mall, 2552 Virginia Avenue, N.W. (Foggy Bottom); 338-4451. Contemporary art by Washington artists.

**Women's National Bank** 1627 K Street, N.W. (downtown); 466-4090. Contemporary art.

**Zenith Gallery** 1441 Rhode Island Avenue, N.W., rear carriage house; 667-3483. Gallery and studios for artists and craftsmen. Member, WADA.

# ART MUSEUMS
See MUSEUMS.

# ART SUPPLIES

**Utrecht Linens** 1250 I Street, N.W.; 898-0555. Branch of the famous artist's supply house in New York. Well-stocked variety.

**Visual Systems** 1727 I Street, N.W. (downtown); 331-7090. Supplies and equipment for graphic art, fine art, drafting, and engineering. Branches in suburbs.

# AUCTIONS, AUCTIONEERS

See ANTIQUES.

# BABYSITTERS

See CHILDREN AND CHILDREN'S THINGS.

# BAKERIES AND PASTRY SHOPS

**Jean-Jacques Fournil** 1220 19th Street, N.W. (Dupont Circle); 466-4264. French bakery. (See listing under RESTAURANTS.)

**French Baker** 1825 I Street, N.W.; 466-4448. Sixteen varieties of bread. Small-scale catering.

**Georgetown Bagelry** 3245 M Street, N.W.; 965-1011 or 965-1012. Thirteen varieties. Sunday–Thursday, 7 AM to 9 PM; Friday–Saturday, 7 AM to midnight.

**Reeves Bakery & Restaurant** 1209 F Street, N.W. (downtown); 347-3781. This Washington landmark is famous not only for its strawberry pie but for its bargain meals, including a perfectly wonderful breakfast bar from 6:45 AM, Monday–Saturday. Conveniently located at Metro Center Metro stop, 12th and F Streets exit and TicketPlace. Closed Sunday.

**Suzanne's** 1735 Connecticut Avenue, N.W. (Dupont Circle); 483-4633. Pastry specialties. (See listings under AFTERNOON TEA; BARS AND PUBS; RESTAURANTS.)

**Vie de France** 1990 K Street, N.W.; 659-0055. Bakery, carryout, and cafe (see listing under RESTAURANTS). Monday–Friday, 7:30 AM–9:30 PM; Saturday, 11 AM–5 PM; closed Sunday.

See also CARRYOUTS AND DELIS.

# BARGAIN AND DISCOUNT STORES

See HABERDASHERIES AND TAILORS; HOME AND KITCHEN FURNISHINGS; JEWELRY; SECONDHAND CLOTHING AND THRIFT SHOPS; WOMEN'S WEAR.

# BARS AND PUBS

Hours are generally daily from 11 AM to 1, 2, or 3 AM. Some places open around 4 PM on weekends. Lower prices for drinks and/or lots of special foods around the cocktail/hungry hour beginning at 5 PM weekdays in most bars. See also NIGHTLIFE; RESTAURANTS. Also refer to "Weekend" on Fridays in the *Washington Post* and to *Washingtonian* magazine.

## Wine Bar

**Suzanne's** 1735 Connecticut Avenue, N.W. (Dupont Circle); 483-4633. A bakery and bistro too. Closed Sunday.

## Capitol Hill

**Bull Feathers** 410 1st Street, S.E.; 543-5005. Victorian style where Hill staffers and lawyers congregate. Parking is easy and near the Capitol South Metro stop.
**Hawk and Dove** 329 Pennsylvania Avenue, S.E.; 543-3300. Typically American bar and grill serving sandwiches, burgers and chefs specials ($5–10). Weekend brunch. Oldies on the jukebox. Three bars separate from the dining area.
**Jenkins Hill** 223 Pennsylvania Avenue, S.E.; 544-6600. Very fashionable Hill bar frequented by tourists, Hill staffers, lawyers, and justices. Dancing Saturday night 9 PM–3 AM. Capitol South Metro stop.
**Kelly's Irish Times Pub** 14 F Street, N.W.; 543-5433. Writers frequent this pub. Beer served in Irish-size pint glasses. Traditional Irish folk music upstairs.

**Tune Inn** 331½ Pennsylvania Avenue, S.E.; 543-2725. Very inexpensive gathering spot for people who live on the Hill; extremely popular for Hill interns. Ham 'n eggs and hamburgers. Good country/western on the jukebox.

## Downtown

**Matt Kane's Bit O' Ireland** 1118 13th Street, N.W.; 638-8058. Upstairs is a real stone bar; traditional Irish folk music. Closed Monday and Sunday. Metro Center Metro stop.

**9:30 Club** 930 F Street, N.W.; concert line: 393-0930. The most extreme punk in town; very colorful. A little bit of every style of popular music. Front bar moderately priced; bar in rear is very fine with excellent champagne selection. Metro Center and Gallery Place Metro stops.

**Post Pub, Inc.** 1422 L Street, N.W.; 628-2111. Very popular with all kinds of newspaper people, from the editors to the typesetters. Reasonable prices and good food.

**Sky Terrace** At the Hotel Washington, 15th Street between Pennsylvania Avenue and F Street, N.W.; 347-4499. A terrific view of Washington. Open from Mother's Day to early October.

## Georgetown

**Au Pied de Cochon** 1335 Wisconsin Avenue, N.W.; 333-5440. Bar and restaurant with very reasonable prices. Open 24 hours except from 2 AM Sunday to 11:30 AM Monday.

**Cafe Med** 3065 M Street, N.W.; 338-0417. Bar popular with Latin Americans. Restaurant with jazz combos, skylights and garden patio. Moderately priced.

**Champions** 1206 Wisconsin Avenue, N.W.; 965-4005. The ultimate sports bar frequented by players and fans from the city's professional sports teams.

**Chelsea's** 1055 Thomas Jefferson Street, N.W.; 298-8222. Pub for dining and dancing. Light menu. Large dance floor and live band. Top 40, oldies, and Latin jazz.

**Garden Terrace** At the Four Seasons Hotel, 2800 Pennsylvania Avenue, N.W.; 342-0444. Piano bar;

pleasant and expensive. *Esquire* said this was one of Washington's four best bars. Tea from 3 to 4:30 PM, weekdays; from 3 to 5, Saturday and Sunday.

**Garrett's** (and Garrett's Restaurant Terrace) 3303 M Street, N.W.; 333-8282. Three bars and separate dining area. Patrons enjoy the different sounds of music here. Happy hour Monday–Friday. Chef's specials vary nightly including seafood and pastas ($4–13).

**J. Paul's** 3218 M Street, N.W.; 333-3450. Dining saloon featuring a raw bar, and daily specials for lunch and dinner with emphasis on fresh seafood. ($7–14)

**Martin's Tavern** 1264 Wisconsin Avenue, N.W.; 333-7370. Mellow bar; gathering place for Georgetown citizens for years. Excellent wholesome American food.

**Mr. Smith's** 3104 M Street, N.W.; 333-3104. This long-established bar has a popular sing-along piano and outdoor garden open year-round.

**Nathan's** 3150 M Street, N.W., at the corner of Wisconsin; 338-2000. Nathan's prides itself on the largest selection of liquor in the city. This is where the case of Canadian Club was hidden. The back room adjacent to the bar is a nice Northern Italian restaurant.

# Dupont Circle/Lower Connecticut Avenue

Bars and pubs abound in this area, each with its own distinctive character; a few are listed here.

**Black Rooster Pub** 1919 L Street, N.W.; 659-4431. Famous for dart-playing. Full dinner menu until 10 PM.

**Brickskeller** 1523 22nd Street, N.W.; 293-1885. The widest selection of beer in town with over 300 domestic and 200 imported varieties. Game room and dining room. For jukebox fans there is a Wurlitzer Bubbler, *c.* 1940, on display. The other jukebox plays swing tunes from the '30s and '40s, some with original labels.

**Chicago Bar & Grill** 1330 19th Street, N.W.; 463-8891. Chicago-style saloon with full-service restaurant serving lunch Monday–Friday, dinner Monday–Saturday, with dancing at 10 PM. Open late. ($8–16)

**El Azteca** 1639 R Street, N.W.; 232-6969. Mexican cantina and lounge of La Fonda Restaurant.

**Fairfax Bar** 2100 Massachusetts Avenue, N.W.; 293-2100. Intimate, expensive, elegant bar with excellent piano and nice fireplace.

**Samantha's** 1823 L Street, N.W.; 223-1823. Bar-restaurant featuring light menu of sandwiches, quiche and chefs specials. Lunch and dinner Monday–Saturday. Disc jockey nightly playing various styles of music.

**Sign of the Whale** 1825 M Street, N.W.; 223-0608. Fin and shellfish specials from a good kitchen. Favorite among singles. Sunday brunch.

**Tabard Inn** 1739 N Street, N.W.; 785-1277. In this mellow, very comfortable, romantic hotel are a couple of rooms with fireplaces where you are welcome to have a drink and wind down. There is a small bar and adjoining restaurant with patio.

## Adams Morgan

This area of the city (18th Street and Columbia Road, N.W.), has come alive with a vibrant mix of cultures.

**Cafe Lautrec** 2431 18th Street, N.W.; 265-6436. Authentic French bistro featuring live music nightly in a casual atmosphere. Thursday–Saturday a tap dancer performs on the bar!

**Millie & Al's** 2440 18th Street, N.W.; 387-8131. A genuine neighborhood bar around for the last 25 years. Pizza and lasagna are favorites. Nice jukebox stocked with a wild mixture of styles.

**Stetson's Tex-Mex Saloon** 1610 U Street, N.W.; 667-6295. Specializing in chili and the best jukebox music; stocked with a wide selection of styles, such as country-western and bebop. Located in the lower Adams Morgan area.

## Maine Avenue Water Street— Southwest

Unique about this area is the view of the waterfront, with houseboats and yachts in the foreground and jets in the background—oh yes, from time to time there's a fantastic sunset, and in April you'll see the cherry blossoms across Washington Channel on Hains Point. The following bars are located within restaurants.

Casa Maria's **Cantina** 700 Water Street, S.W.; 554-5302. Happy hour with an all-you-can-eat buffet of Mexican foods Monday through Friday, 4–8 PM.

Gangplank's **Lower Lounge** and **Tower** (for the sun-

set) 600 Water Street, S.W.; 554-5000. Less touristy and relatively quiet compared to the other bars in the area. Happy hour Monday through Friday, 4–7 PM.
Pier Seven's **Engine Room** 650 Water Street, S.W.; 554-2500. Features a live trio. Happy hour includes free hors d'oeuvres and raw bar at slight charge Monday through Friday, 4:30–6:30 PM.

# BED AND BREAKFAST

Listed below are *reservation service organizations* (RSOs). These organizations help you by confirming your reservation and inspecting the private homes listed with them. Homes are chosen based on cleanliness, comfortable rooms, graceful and friendly hosts, and proximity to public transportation. A continental breakfast is included. All rates are subject to 10% sales tax and $1/room/night occupancy tax in Washington; rates in the suburbs are subject to similar taxes. *Note*: The busiest months of the year are April, May, June, and October.

**Bed & Breakfast League** 3639 Van Ness Street, N.W., Washington, D.C. 20008; 202/363-7767. Represents about 60 private homes and apartments in and around Washington. With a few exceptions, a 2-night minimum stay is required. A $25 nonrefundable deposit is required, to receive a written confirmation of your reservation. Payment may be made by personal check, Visa, MasterCard, or American Express. Singles, $30–55/night; doubles, $45–70/night.

**Bed 'n Breakfast, Ltd. of Washington, D.C.** P.O. Box 12011, Washington, D.C. 20005; 202/328-3510. Represents about 80 private homes in Washington and the suburbs. Comment cards are mailed with each confirmed reservation. A $40 deposit is required 2 weeks prior to the reservation. Payment may be made by personal check, Visa, MasterCard, or American Express. Singles, $30–75/night; doubles, $40–85/night.

**Sweet Dreams and Toast** P.O. Box 4835-0035, Washington, D.C. 20008; 202/483-9191. Represents about 100 private homes in Northwest Washington and Capitol Hill; Chevy Chase and Bethesda, Maryland; Falls

Church, Alexandria, and Arlington in Northern Virginia; and Annapolis, Maryland. A 2-night minimum stay is required. A $50 deposit is required when booking the reservation; balance due 10 days prior to arrival. Payment may be made by personal check, Visa, or MasterCard. Singles, $40–60/night; doubles, $53–70/night.

Sweet Dreams and Toast publishes a list by state of bed and breakfast organizations (representing private homes) and related publications for the United States, such as B&B cookbooks and books advertising accommodations. The 1986 list is available by sending $3 and a self-addressed stamped envelope to Sweet Dreams and Toast.

*Note*: Also see Adams Inn, Georgetown Dutch Inn, Gralyn, Normandy Inn, and Tabard Inn listed under HOTELS AND MOTELS.

# BICYCLES AND BICYCLING

Washington is blessed with miles of bicycle paths—through the Rock Creek Park, around Hains Point, among the monuments, along the Canal Towpath to Harpers Ferry, if you wish, and into Alexandria down to Mount Vernon along the George Washington Memorial Parkway. Because bicycling is a very popular sport, there are a number of associations that offer valuable publications and have tours:

## Associations and Their Publications

**American Youth Hostel, Potomac Area Council** 1017 K Street, N.W., 2nd floor (McPherson Square or Metro Center Metro stop, 11th Street exit); 783-4943. Information on hostel membership and hiking, canoeing, skiing, *and* bicycling—locally, around the country, and around the world, including national and international bicycling trips. Travel shop with discounts to members offers travel books, reflective gear, helmets, and lots of related items. The *Greater Washington Area Bicycle Atlas* is available here for $6.95 + $1 for postage and handling. Quarterly newsletter lists all trips and activities for the Potomac Area Council; write P.O. Box 28607, Central Station, Washington, D.C. 20038.

**D.C. Government Office of Documents** District Building, 14th Street and Pennsylvania Avenue, N.W., Room 19, Washington, D.C. 20004 (Federal Triangle Metro stop); 727-5090. Find here *Getting Around Washington by Bicycle*, an 8-section map printed on waterproof paper, including a 44-page guidebook that tells how to get over the bridges. Just $3! Stop by Monday–Friday, 9 AM–4 PM, or order by mail with payment enclosed made payable to D.C. Treasurer.

**Metropolitan Washington Council of Governments** *Bicycle Routes in the Washington Area* is a 3-color map showing 400 miles of signed routes, both on- and off-road paths, and includes the East Coast Bicycle Trail and Metrorail stations. $5 by mail or in person at COG's Information Center, 1875 I Street, N.W., Suite 200, Washington, D.C. 20006; 223-6800, ext. 230. Office hours Monday–Friday, 1–5 PM.

**Potomac Pedalers Touring Club** Box 23601, Washington, D.C. 20026; 363-6687 (informative recorded message or call Thursday evenings). "Pedal Patter" newsletter; tours are categorized by level of biking ability. Included in membership services is the counsel of an effective cycling instructor, who will discuss all matters of bicycling.

**Washington Area Bicyclist Association** 530 7th Street, S.E., 20003 (between E and G Streets and 2 blocks south of Eastern Market Metro stop); 544-5349. Office hours Monday–Friday, 9 AM–6 PM. Membership: $10, student or low-income; $15, individual; $25, family; $30, corporate. Newsletter and monthly meetings; Pedal Pull hotline; bicycle commuting assistance. Bike route of the Washington Area, $3.50 by mail. *Greater Washington Area Bicycle Atlas* (for intermediate and advanced bikers), $6.95 + $1 for postage and handling. "Consumer's Guide to Bicycle Helmets," free with self-addressed stamped envelope.

## Rentals, Sales, and Repairs

**Big Wheel Bikes** 1004 Vermont Avenue, N.W. at K Street (McPherson Square Metro stop); 638-3301; Monday–Saturday, 10 AM–6 PM. Also at 1034 33rd Street, N.W. (Georgetown); 337-0254; Monday–Sunday, 10 AM–6 PM. Repairs while open at both locations but they'll probably take more than one day. Bicycles, mopeds, scooters, and accessories; bicycle rentals. Branch in Bethesda, Maryland.

**Fletcher's Boat House** Canal and Reservoir Roads, N.W.; 244-0461. Located on the Canal Towpath. Bicycle as well as boat rentals. Seasonal hours.

**Metropolis Bike & Scooter, Inc.** 719 8th Street, S.E. (Capitol Hill, Eastern Market Metro stop); 543-8900. Monday–Wednesday and Friday, 11 AM–7 PM; Thursday, 11–9; Saturday, 10–6; Sunday, 10:30–5. Repair shop open same hours as salesroom. Prompt, efficient, and courteous service on all brands. Branch in the Shirlington Shopping Mall, Arlington, Virginia.

**Thompson's Boat Center** Virginia Avenue and Rock Creek Parkway (across from the Watergate); 333-4861. Bicycle as well as boat rentals. Seasonal hours.

## Races, Etc.

**Annual Bike for Sight** Five-mile ride around the Tidal Basin in April, 9 AM–noon, for the benefit of the Prevention of Blindness Society of Metropolitan Washington, 1775 Church Street, N.W., 20035; 234-1010. Register by mail or on the day of the event at 8:30 AM, south ballfield. Listen and watch for announcements.

**HEY-BIKE** 439-2453. Recorded message giving information on current biking trips and races.

**National Capital Open Bicycle Race** Usually the third weekend in April. Attracts international teams in 6 races of varying lengths. Held on the Ellipse just south of the White House. For information, call 864-2211, or HEY-BIKE for recorded message.

For other biking activities, check the "Sporting Life" column in the "Weekend" section of Friday's *Washington Post*.

# BOATING ON THE POTOMAC

Certain areas of the Potomac River and C&O Canal are safe for canoeing and rowing. Paddleboating can be done at the Tidal Basin.

**Fletcher's Boat House** 4940 Canal Road, N.W. (Canal and Reservoir Road); 244-0461. Canoes and rowboats for use on the C&O Canal along the towpath or on the Potomac River.

**Jack's Boats** 3500 K Street, N.W. (under Key Bridge); 337-9642. Canoes and rowboats for use on the Potomac River. Seasonal hours.

**Thompson Boat Center** Rock Creek Parkway and Virginia Avenue, N.W. (opposite the Watergate in Foggy Bottom); 333-4861. Canoes, rowboats, and "sails" for use on the Potomac River. Seasonal hours.

**Tidal Basin** North side. Canoes and paddleboats.

For additional boating activities, check the "Sporting Life" column in the "Weekend" section of Friday's *Washington Post*.

# BOOKS, BOOKSHOPS, AND BOOK SALES

## Bookshops

Washington's bookshops are scattered all over the city. A few of the more personal shops are listed in this guide. Consult the D.C. Yellow Pages for bookshops that specialize in cookbooks, religious topics, arts and crafts, comics, mysteries and science fiction, professional/technical topics, foreign languages, natural history, Shakespeare, the classics, hypnotism, and preservation because whatever obscure topic you may be interested in, Washington probably has a bookshop to satisfy your curiosity. You will also find a select group of fine books in most of Washington's museums. Don't miss the ones at the Lincoln Memorial and in the Bell Tower of the Old Post Office Building.

**Audubon Book Shop** 1621 Wisconsin Avenue, N.W. (Georgetown); 337-6062. Specializing in natural history; you will also find bird feeders and bug boxes!

**Backstage, Inc.** 2101 P Street, N.W. (Dupont Circle Metro stop); 775-1488. The performing arts store. Besides books about all aspects of the performing arts, there are posters, scripts, sheet music, a full line of costumes and makeup, dance wear, and special programs, such as makeup demonstrations.

**Booked Up** 1209 31st Street, N.W. (Georgetown); 965-3244. Fine rare and unusual and first edition books.

**Calliope** 3424 Connecticut Avenue, N.W.; 365-0111. Specializing in literature.

**Cheshire Cat** 5512 Connecticut Avenue, N.W. (between Livingston and Morrison); 244-3956. Especially for children and parents. Saturday mornings in the fall and spring authors discuss and autograph their books.

**Common Concerns** 1347 Connecticut Avenue, N.W. (Dupont Circle); 463-6500. Specializes in black studies and the Third World; also T-shirts, posters, etc.

**Francis Scott Key Book Shop** 28th and O Streets, N.W. (Georgetown); 337-4144. Fiction, nonfiction, and children's books; will special order.

**Franz Bader, Inc.** Bookshop and gallery, 1701 Pennsylvania Avenue, N.W. (downtown); 659-5515. Art, architecture, and German books; very good selection. Closed Sunday and Monday.

**Geological Survey, U.S. Government** 1800 F Street, N.W., Room 1028 (downtown); 343-8073. Maps and books. Monday–Friday, 8:15 AM–3:45 PM.

**Government Printing Office** North Capitol Street between G and H Streets, N.W. (downtown); 783-3238; Monday–Friday, 8 AM–4 PM. Bookstores also at Department of Commerce, 14th Street and Constitution Avenue, N.W., 377-3527, Monday–Friday, 8 AM–4 PM; and in the Matomic Building, 1717 H Street, N.W., 653-5075, Monday–Friday, 9 AM–5 PM. To order by mail, write to Superintendent of Documents, U.S. Government Printing Office, Washington, D.C. 20402.

**Books**

**International Learning Center** 1715 Connecticut Avenue, N.W. (Dupont Circle Metro stop, Q Street exit); 232-4111. Foreign-language dictionaries, grammar books, cassettes, newspapers and magazines, games, and children's books. Also, major travel guides, maps, and books on histories and policies of foreign countries.

**Kramer Books & Afterwords** 1517 Connecticut Avenue, N.W. (Dupont Circle); 387-1400. Café in back. And branches.

**Lambda Rising** 1625 Connecticut Avenue, N.W. (Dupont Circle Metro stop, Q Street exit); 462-6969. Gay and lesbian literature. Also, community-support bulletin board, newsletter, mail-order catalog, and author programs.

**The Lantern, A Bryn Mawr Bookshop** 2803 M Street, N.W.; 333-2803. Used books sold for the benefit of scholarships to Bryn Mawr. Many topics, including children's books.

**Map Store** 1636 I Street, N.W. (Farragut West Metro stop, 17th Street exit, or Farragut North Metro stop); 628-2608. Everything from city maps to world atlases. Closed Saturdays except during December.

**Moonstone Bookcellars** 2145 Pennsylvania Avenue, N.W. (Foggy Bottom); Specializes in science fiction, fantasy, and mystery.

**National Gallery of Art Bookstore** Main shop is in the West Building; 842-6466. Wide selection of art books, reproductions, and cards.

**Olsson's Books & Records** 1239 Wisconsin Avenue, N.W. (Georgetown); 338-9544. Also at 1340 Connecticut Avenue, N.W. (Dupont Circle); 785-1133. The *Washingtonian* has said that this is where the best stock can be found.

**Politics and Prose** 5010 Connecticut Avenue, N.W.; 364-1919. Open every day, this is a place to come to talk about books; authors visit Sundays at noon. Political and literary magazines also.

**Reiter's** 2120 Pennsylvania Avenue, N.W. (Foggy Bottom); 223-3327. Their specialty is standard medical, professional, scientific, and technical texts, dictionaries, and a wide variety of reference books.

**Second Story Books** 2000 P Street, N.W. (Dupont Circle); 659-8884. Rare, used, and out-of-print books and records; appraisals; and search service.

**Smithsonian Bookstore** National Museum of American History, Constitution Avenue at 14th Street, N.W. (on the Mall); 357-1784. Books also sold in all the museums of the Smithsonian.

**Travel Merchandise Mart** 1435 K Street, N.W. (McPherson Square Metro stop); 371-6656. Travel agency, travel ware, and bookstore, with a good selection of Washington guides and maps.

**Waldenbooks** 17th Street and Pennsylvania Avenue, N.W. (downtown); 393-1490. This branch has a foreign-language center, including German, French, Spanish, Italian, Chilean, Argentinean, and British magazines and newspapers. Also at 409 12th Street, N.W. (downtown); 638-0225; and in Georgetown Park at M Street and Wisconsin Avenue; 333-8033.

**Washington Project for the Arts (WPA)** 404 7th Street, N.W. (downtown); 347-8304. Imaginative selection including handmade books.

**Yes! Bookshop** 1035 31st Street, N.W. (Georgetown); 338-7874. Specializing in inner development and holistic health.

# Guides to Washington

Listed below are some of the most recent guides to Washington and a few of the "classics," which may be available only in Washington bookstores and libraries. The reader is also referred to publications of the Information Center for Handicapped Individuals (see HANDICAPPED INDIVIDUALS' RESOURCES).

*Best Restaurants and Others, Washington, D.C. and Environs*, by Phyllis Chasanow-Richman. 101 Productions, 1985. $4.95.

*Capital Entertaining: Caterers to Call and Places to Party in and around Washington, D.C.*, by Polmer and Yonkers. 101 Productions, 1985. $6.95.

*Fairs & Festivals: A Smithsonian Guide to Celebrations in Maryland, Virginia and Washington, D.C.*, by E. R. Gilbert. Smithsonian Institution Press, 1982. Paperbound, $4.50.

*Flashmaps, The Instant Guide to Washington*. Flashmaps Publications, Inc. Revised edition. Paperbound, $4.95.

*Fodor's Washington, D.C. and Vicinity*. Fodor's Modern Guides, 1986. $7.95.

*Frommer's Washington, D.C. and Historic Virginia on $40 a Day/1986–87.* Simon & Schuster, 1986. $10.95.

*A Guide to the Architecture of Washington, D.C.: Twenty Walking and Motoring Tours of Washington and Vicinity,* by Cox, et al., for the Washington Metropolitan Chapter of the American Institute of Architects. McGraw-Hill, 1987.

*I Love Washington Guide,* by Marilyn J. Appleberg. Macmillan, 1982. Paperbound, $4.95.

*A Museum Guide to Washington,* by Betty Ross. The collection of *every* museum and art gallery in Washington is discussed in detail, including history of the museum and collection, and architectural details of the building itself. Illustrated, with index and bibliography. Americana Press, P.O. Box 9747, Washington, D.C. 20016, 1986. $9.95 + $1.50 postage and handling.

*Natural Washington: A Nature-Lover's Guide to the Parks, Wildlife Sanctuaries, Hiking and Bicycling Trails, Swamps, Zoos, [etc.] Within a 50-Mile Radius of Washington, D.C.,* by Bill and Phyllis Thomas. Holt, Rinehart, Winston, 1980. Paperbound, $6.95.

*Official Guide to the Smithsonian.* Smithsonian Institution Press, 1981. Paperbound, $2.95.

*One-Day Trips to Beauty and Bounty: More Than 150 Excursions Within a Day's Drive of Washington, D.C.,* by Jane Ockershausen Smith. EPM Publications, Inc., 1003 Turkey Run Road, McLean, Virginia 22101. Paperbound, $9.95.

*Outdoor Sculpture of D.C.,* by James Goode. Smithsonian Institution Press, 1974. $12.50.

*Pathfinder Pathguide to the Nation's Capital.* Maps and directions for walking tours. Pathfinder Tour Consultants, Box 318, Olney, Maryland 20832, 1985. $4.95.

*Spring in Washington,* by Louis J. Halle. Atheneum, 1963. Paperbound, $1.25.

*A Walking Guide to Historic Georgetown.* This contains the best map of Georgetown you will find. Historic Georgetown, Inc., 1971. Paperbound, $2.50.

*Washington, D.C., The Complete Guide,* by Duffield, Kramer & Shepherd. Random House, 1982. Paperbound, $7.95.

*Washington Itself, An Informal Guide to the Capital of the United States,* by E. J. Applewhite. Warm, per-

sonal commentary. Alfred A. Knopf, 1981. Paperbound, $8.95.
*Washington on Foot.* Smithsonian Institution Press,
1984. Paperbound, $4.95.

## Articles

These articles are well worth reading:
"The Celebrated City," *The Washington Post Maga-
zine*, in Sunday's *Washington Post*, February 2, 1986.
*Washington Post* writers and editors examine how
Washington has grown and developed over the past
25 years.
"Hometown Washington, D.C." *National Geographic*,
January 1983, Vol. 163, no. 1. Includes many photo-
graphs and a map of tourist Washington.

A newcomer's or insider's guide appears in each
March issue of the *Washingtonian* magazine. Includes
tips on neighborhoods, restaurants, schools, nightlife,
sports, theater tickets, auto stickers, etc.

## Books about Washington, Its Life and Times, Politics and History, and Its Beauty

*Above Washington*, by Robert Cameron. A bird's-eye
view of this beautiful city. Cameron, 1982. $19.95.
*The Brethren: Inside the Supreme Court*, by Bob Woodward and Scott Armstrong. The Supreme Court from
1969 to 1976. Simon & Schuster, 1979. $12.95; pap-
erbound, 1980, $3.50.
*Howard Baker's Washington: An Intimate Portrait of
the Nation's Capital City*. Candid photos of world leaders taken by the former senator from Tennessee. Norton, 1982. $19.95.
*The Library of Congress: Architecture and Decora-
tions*, by Herbert Small, edited by Henry Hope Reed.
Symbolism and significance of the late Victorian decorative devices seen in the Jefferson Building. Norton,
1982. $19.50; paperbound, $6.50.
*One Day in Washington*, by the National Press Photographers Association, Region XI Staff. Madrona
Publishers, 1985. $19.95.

*Our Neighbors on Lafayette Square: Anecdotes and Reminiscences*, by Benjamin Ogle Taylor. The author, the son of the builder of Octagon House, for many years lived by himself on Lafayette Square. Republished by the Junior League of Washington, 1982. $5.

*Privileged Communication, The Nixon Years*, by John D. Ehrlichman. Simon & Schuster, 1981. $14.95.

*Washington, The Capital*. A photo essay. Foreword by Clement Conger and photography by Robert Llewellyn. Thomasson-Grant Publishing Co., Charlottesville, Virginia 22901, 1981. Hardback, $28.

*Washington, D.C.*, by J. C. Suares with text by Bill Harris. Photographs (160) showing how quiet and peaceful this city can be. Abrams, 1982. $50.

*Washington, Design of the Federal City*. National Archives and Records Service. Acropolis Books, Ltd., 1981. Paperbound, $7.95.

*Washington: Houses of the Capital*, by Derry Moore (photographer) and Henry Mitchell (writer). Viking, 1982. $40.

*Washington Week in Review*, by Paul Duke, et al. Warner Books, 1986. Paperbound, $9.95.

*Waters of Potowmack*, by Paul Metcalf. Chronicle of life along the Potomac culled from original records. North Point Press, 1982. $17.75.

## Stories Set in Washington

*Advise and Consent*, by Allen Drury. Pulitzer prize-winning novel of Washington politics. Book of the Month Club selection. Doubleday, 1959. $16.95.

*The Company*, by John Erlichman. Fast-paced novel about the Executive Branch, the CIA, and the FBI. Simon & Schuster, 1976. $8.95.

*Fool's Mercy*, by Henry Allen. Thriller set in Washington. Carroll & Graf, 1984. Paperbound, $3.95.

*Madonna Red*, by James Carroll. Suspense: problems of Catholic doctrine in the modern world concern a priest, cardinal, and nun; Belfast terrorist heads for Washington to assassinate an official of the British Embassy during a ceremony in the Cardinal's Cathedral. Little, Brown, 1976. $7.95.

*Murder on Capitol Hill*, by Margaret Truman. Arbor House, 1981.

*Murder in the White House*, by Margaret Truman. Arbor House, 1980. $9.95.

## Book Sales

**Association of American Foreign Service Women Book Fair** Held usually in the fall at the State Department, 23rd and C Streets, N.W. (use 23rd Street entrance). Benefits scholarship fund and community projects. Donations are tax deductible. Books, art and artifacts, stamps, children's literature and foreign languages. For further information and free pickup, call 223-5796.

**Brandeis University National Women's Committee Book Sale** Usually held in the spring in downtown Washington for one week. Proceeds from selling the old books are used to purchase new books for the Brandeis University Library, thus their motto "new books for old." The D.C. Public School Libraries have first choice in purchasing books at the sale and any books not sold are given to prisons. All donations are tax deductible. For free pickup, call 229-9143 and leave message.

**Goodwill Annual Booksale** Usually held between late October and early December. In 1983 it was held at the Convention Center with in excess of 100,000 books for sale. For up-to-date information call Davis Memorial Goodwill, 636-4225.

**Vassar College Book Sale** Usually held in the early spring for a week. Sales benefit the scholarship fund for area students. Donations of books, records and art accepted year-round. For free pickup, call 301/299-4855. Watch newspaper ads for dates and location of sale.

# BUSES

See TRANSPORTATION.

# CABS

See TRANSPORTATION.

# CALENDAR OF EVENTS

See ANNUAL EVENTS; INFORMATION.

# CANDY

See CHOCOLATE AND CANDY.

# CARRYOUTS AND DELIS

Most carryouts and delis cater to those working early in the morning, so you can count on their being open by 7:30 AM at least, Monday–Friday. Thus "open early" means that they open earlier than 7:30 AM. Most of them close by 4 PM or so; "open late" means open through the dinner hours at least. On Saturdays and Sundays, if they open at all, it is usually from 10 or 11 AM.

**Amber Grain Store** 2313 Wisconsin Avenue, N.W. (north Georgetown); 333-4951. Freshly made salads, sandwiches, prepared gourmet foods for carryout (such as whole melting brie wrapped in brioche), homemade cheesecake, and an assortment of sorbet, frozen yogurt, soft drinks, and fruit juice. This is the retail part of the catering business known as American Amber Grain, Fruited Plain & Shining Sea Co.! Hours are Monday–Friday, 8 AM–8 PM; Saturday, 10 AM–4 PM.

**Bon Apetit** 2040 I Street, N.W.; 452-0055. Twenty-one varieties of hamburgers and other nice things. Very popular. Open early weekdays and 'til midnight every night of the week.

**C.F. Folk's** 1225 19th Street, N.W.; 293-0162. Each day of the week fresh creative specialties are prepared featuring an ethnic cuisine such as Cajun, Mexican, Indian, Italian, Middle Eastern, and All-American. Outside patio and about 18 seats inside. Catering and delivery services. Opera music in the background. Monday–Friday, 11:45 AM–3 PM.

**Dahlia's** 1134 19th Street, N.W.; 429-9307. Full range of creative daily specials including salads, desserts and locally made ice cream. Emphasis on fresh, preservative-free ingredients without a lot of filler. Mayonnaise is homemade. Catering services. Benches outdoors, weather permitting. Monday–Friday, 7:30 AM–5:30 PM.

**Deli of Capitol Hill** 332 Pennsylvania Avenue, S.E.; 547-8668. Homemade blintzes, soups, salads, beef stew, stuffed cabbage, etc. Open 'til 10 PM weekdays; Saturday, Sunday, 9 AM–4 PM.

**Fast & Fresh** 600 Maryland Avenue, S.W.; 554-7870. Bakery, cafeteria, and carryout. Open 'til 9 PM weekdays; Saturday, 9 AM–4 PM; closed Sunday. (Saturday, cafeteria only.)

**French Bread Factory** 3222 N Street, N.W.; 338-7776. Carryout sandwiches, croissants, salads, pastries; soup and daily specials such as meat, fish, or chicken dishes. Open 'til 10 PM weekdays and Saturday; Sunday, open 7:30 AM–7 PM.

**Loeb's** 832 15th Street, N.W.; 737-2071. The perfect New York deli, serving kosher-style breakfast and lunch. Their chopped chicken liver has an excellent rating. Closed weekends and legal holidays.

**Negril Bakery and Carry-Out** 2437 18th Street, N.W. (Adams Morgan); 232-8555. Jamaican delicacies. Open 'til 8 PM Monday–Saturday; 'til 5 PM Sunday.

**Prego Deli** 210 7th Street, S.E.; 547-8686. Excellent subs, fresh pasta, salads, meatloaf, sausage, homemade soups, cheeses, etc. Open 'til 7 PM Monday–Saturday; closed Sunday.

**So's Your Mom** 1831 Columbia Road, N.W. (Adams Morgan); 462-3666. Typical New York deli featuring smoked lox, bagels, pasta salads, croissants and desserts; many items directly from New York and Baltimore. Catering service. Monday–Saturday, 8 AM–8 PM; Sunday, 8 AM–2 PM.

**Take Me Home** 3212 O Street, N.W.; 298-6818. An imaginative gourmet sandwich shop and catering service with such creations as corned beef with walnut horseradish sauce; smoked turkey with lingonberries, or tuna with apple and green peppercorns on such breads as whole-wheat pecan, cheddar dill, or pumpernickel, all homemade. Closed Sunday.

**Young's Carryout** YWCA Building, 624 9th Street,

**Carryouts**

N.W.; 737-2111. Snack bar and carryout. Licensed to sell the famous YWCA chocolate chip cookies.

See also BAKERIES AND PASTRY SHOPS; RESTAURANTS.

# CARS

See TRANSPORTATION.

# CHEESE SHOPS

**Sutton Place Gourmet** 3201 New Mexico Avenue, N.W. (near American University); 363-5800. Over 300 varieties of cheese.

See also GOURMET FOODS AND MARKETS; WINES AND LIQUORS.

# CHILDREN AND CHILDREN'S THINGS

## Carousels

**Glen Echo Park** has the best carousel, complete with large band organ and brass ring (on display). It has been in this park since 1921. The handcarved and painted wooden figures and canopy were done by the Dentzel Co. of Philadelphia. It operates May through September, Wednesdays from 10–2 and weekends, noon to 6 PM; 492-6282. Rides are 25¢.

**On the Mall** near the Arts Industries Building, this carousel has a variety of 60 animals. Open Tuesdays through Sundays, weather permitting, late April through September; beginning June, open Monday also; 357-2700. Rides are 50¢.

**Washington Cathedral** has its wonderful completely restored antique carousel with piano-roll music in operation whenever there is a festival going on. (See ANNUAL EVENTS.) Fee charged.

# Clothes and Toy Shops

A few of the specialty shops are listed; see also DE-PARTMENT STORES; TOYS.

**Cheshire Cat Children's Book Store** 5512 Connecticut Avenue, N.W.; 244-3956. Lovely selection in this small shop neary Chevy Chase Circle and just north of Livingston Street, N.W.

**Esther Shop-Growing Up** 1207 F Street, N.W. (downtown); 347-1536. Also at Mazza Gallerie, Wisconsin and Western Avenues, N.W.; 244-7206. Infants to size 16 for boys and size 14 for girls. Clothes, toys, puppets. Import and domestic labels.

**F.A.O. Schwarz** Georgetown Park at Wisconsin and M Streets, N.W.; 342-2285. Also at Mazza Gallerie at Wisconsin and Western Avenues, N.W.; 363-8455. Branches of the famous New York City store, carrying unique imported and domestic toys for all ages.

**Francis-Reilly, Inc.** 1361 Wisconsin Avenue, N.W. (Georgetown); 333-7166. *The* children's shop in Georgetown. Children's sizes infants to 12. Steiff animals, imported English coats, Florence Eiseman clothes, etc.

**Just Shoes** 3301 New Mexico Avenue, N.W., at Foxhall Square (near American University); 244-2224. Unique domestic and imported shoes for infants and young children.

**Just So** 3301 New Mexico Avenue, N.W., at Foxhall Square (near American University); 244-0500. Sizes infants to girls size 14 and to boys size 7. Mainly clothes—American and import labels—and gift items.

**Little Sprout of Georgetown** 3222 M Street, N.W. (Georgetown Park); 342-2273. Clothes with character, in newborn size to 14/16 for girls and boys. Also toys, mobiles, and wall hangings.

**Phineas Frog and Friends** 210 7th Street, S.E. (Capitol Hill); 543-1686. Imaginative toys and gifts, including reasonably priced party favors, helium-filled balloons, and Brio toys.

**Red Balloon** 1073 Wisconsin Avenue, N.W. (just below M Street in Georgetown); 965-1200. Imported and domestic clothing and toys.

**Tree Top Toys, Inc.** 3301 New Mexico Avenue, N.W., at Foxhall Square (near American University); 244-3500. Ingenious items for children, such as a sun shield for use in cars.

## Day-Care and Sitting Services

Day-care facilities are listed in the Yellow Pages under Day Nurseries and Child Care. The following organization may be of help in choosing a day-care center:

**Washington Child Development Council** 2121 Decatur Place, N.W., Washington, D.C. 20008; 387-0002. Information referral service for local day-care facilities. Day-care advocacy in the Washington area. The council conducts training seminars on early childhood issues.

**Sitters Unlimited** Nancy L. Richards, Franchise Owner, Washington, D.C./Northern Virginia Area, 205 Yoakum Parkway, #1505, Alexandria, Va. 22304; 703/823-0888. Licensed agency with services on an hourly, daily, or extended basis in your hotel or home. Convention day-care services can be arranged, as well as tours for children on an individual or a group basis. Brochure available by mail or at the Tourist Information Center (see INFORMATION).

## Entertainment

Events in the Washington area for children are listed in the *Washington Post*'s "Weekend" section "Carousel" column, published every Friday, and in the *Washingtonian* magazine, published monthly.

**Adventure Theatre** Glen Echo Park, Md., on MacArthur Boulevard at Goldsboro Road; 320-5331. Performances practically every weekend. Admission charged. Glen Echo publishes a free quarterly announcement of classes and performances, which is sent to persons on their mailing list.

**Capital Children's Museum Shows** 800 3rd Street, N.E. (Capitol Hill); 543-8600. Variety of live performances throughout the year usually held on Friday, Saturday, and Sunday. Admission charged. Free newsletter sent to persons on their mailing list.

**Children's Radio Theater** Carried on WPFW radio, 89.3 FM, Saturdays, 8 to 9 AM. Listeners participate in a call-in following each program. 783-3104.

**Dial-a-Story** 638-5717.

**Films for Young People** Hirshhorn Museum & Sculpture Garden, 7th Street and Independence Avenue, S.W. (on the Mall); 357-2700. Saturdays about 11 AM. Free admission.

**John F. Kennedy Center for the Performing Arts**
*Black History Month in February*: month-long festival of activities for children. *Imagination Celebration*: week before and week following Easter. *Programs for Children and Youth, Fall Season*: September through December. Performances in each series are given Friday night, Saturday morning, and Sunday afternoon in the Theatre Lab and Terrace Theater on the Terrace level. For each of these series of programs, request a brochure one month in advance of the programming by calling 254-3600. The brochure describes the shows and how to order tickets, many of which are free.

**Saturday Morning at the National** Helen Hayes Gallery, 1321 Pennsylvania Avenue; 783-3372. Theater for children of all ages, at 9:30 and 11 each Saturday morning, September through May. Free; reservations recommended.

**Smithsonian Discovery Theatre** Smithsonian Arts and Industries Building, 900 Jefferson Drive, S.W.; 357-1500. Performances Tuesday through Saturday. Shows vary from month to month and include theater, dance, puppetry, etc. Admission charged. Request an announcement of performances by calling the above number.

# Museums

Many of Washington's museums are suitable for children; see also MUSEUMS. The following are of special interest; 3 of them have hands-on exhibits.

**Capital Children's Museum** 800 3rd Street, N.E. (Capitol Hill); 543-8600. Touch and play with all exhibits; interesting computer room. Closed major holidays; otherwise open daily, 10 AM–5 PM. Admission charged.

**Claude Moore Colonial Farm at Turkey Run** 6310 Old Georgetown Pike, McLean, Va. 22101; 703/442-7557. Twenty-five minutes from Washington. (See directions under EXCURSIONS FROM THE CITY.) This outdoors working farm depicts a typical poor farm of the 1770s. April through December, Wednesday–Sunday, 10 AM–4:30 PM. Adults, $1; children under 12, 50¢.

**DAR Museum, Discovery Hall** 1776 D Street, N.W.; 628-1776. A quiet space just for children from ages 4 to 13 who are interested in early American household wares, toys, and other colonial paraphernalia. Weekdays, 9–4; Sunday, 1–5; closed Saturday. Free.

**Family Tours at the National Gallery of Art** Constitution Avenue at 6th Street, N.W.; 842-6249. Reservations required. Saturday mornings from 10 to 11:30. Groups of about 20 persons have individual instructors. Suitable for families with children at least 6 years of age.

**Smithsonian Institution Discovery Room, Naturalist Center and Insect Zoo** National Museum of Natural History (on the Mall); 357-2700. For free ticket information, see MUSEUMS—HISTORICAL AND SCIENTIFIC, Smithsonian section.

**Washington Doll's House and Toy Museum** 5236 44th Street, N.W. (near Wisconsin and Western Avenues, N.W., and Mazza Gallerie shopping mall, one block west of Wisconsin Avenue between Jenifer and Harrison Streets); 244-0024. A museum of nostalgia exhibiting a carefully researched collection of doll's houses, dolls, and antique toys. Dollhouse furniture and accessories for sale. Inquire about catered parties in the museum's party room. Tuesday–Saturday, 10–5; Sunday, noon to 5. Closed Monday, Thanksgiving, Christmas, and New Year's Day. Admission charged.

# Playgrounds and Parks

A most comprehensive list of activities for children appears in "Kiosk," a monthly calendar of Washington area events of the National Park Service (see INFORMATION—CALENDAR OF EVENTS). For up-to-the-minute information, call Dial-a-Park, 426-6975.

**Candy Cane City** Rock Creek Park, Beach Drive at East-West Highway. Swings and play equipment.

**Hains Point** East Potomac Park, Ohio Drive, beside the Potomac River. Swings and play equipment.

**Montrose Park** R Street, N.W. at 31st. Swings and play equipment.

**National Zoological Park** 3001 Connecticut Avenue, N.W., or Beach Drive, in Rock Creek Park; 673-4800. See ZOOS for detailed information.

**Peirce Mill in Rock Creek Park** 2375 Tilden Street, N.W., at Beach Drive; 426-6908. A working flour mill built by Isaac Peirce in 1820 with Oliver Evans-type machinery. According to seasonal availability, corn, wheat, rye, oats, and buckwheat are ground into 27 varieties of flour, which are sold in cloth bags. Mill open Wednesday–Sunday, 8–4:30; grinding Saturdays and Sundays, 1 PM. Miller and assistants wear period clothing, and from time to time there are special related activities.

**Rock Creek Park Nature Center** 5200 Glover Road, N.W. at Military Road; 426-6829. Open Tuesday–Sunday, 9–5. Inquire about times of planetarium shows and guided walks on weekends.

**Theodore Roosevelt Island** Accessible only from the Virginia side of the Potomac River. Cross Roosevelt Bridge at the west end of Constitution Avenue and take the George Washington Memorial Parkway north; the parking area is immediately on your right. Cross a footbridge to the island. Nature walks.

In the winter, enjoy *ice skating* outdoors. (See SKATING.) See also EXCURSIONS FROM THE CITY for suitable one-day trips for children, such as Baltimore, Maryland; Flying Circus, Bealeton, Virginia; Mount Vernon, Virginia, and Sugar Loaf Mountain, Comus, Maryland.

# CHOCOLATE AND CANDY

**Chez Chocolate** 1101 Connecticut Avenue, N.W.; 833-3250.

**Chocolate, Chocolate** Georgetown Park, 3222 M Street, N.W.; 338-3356. Hungarian and Swiss chocolate truffles, Belgian chocolates, and other delicacies.

**Georgetown Coffee Tea and Spice** 1330 Wisconsin Avenue, N.W.; 338-3801. A magnificent selection of hard candies.

**Krön Chocolatier** Mazza Gallerie at Wisconsin and Western Avenues, N.W.; 966-4946. Delicious Hungarian chocolates.

**Velati's Caramels at Woodward & Lothrop** 11th and G Streets, N.W. (downtown); 347-5300, ext. 2221. When the original Velati's shop was torn down, the business moved to Woodies. Woodies also sells Godiva, Perugina, and diet candies.

# CHURCHES

See RELIGIOUS SERVICES; SIGHTS WORTH SEEING-OTHER SIGHTS.

# COFFEE AND TEA

**Daily Grind** 1613 Connecticut Avenue, N.W.; 265-3348. Coffees, teas, spices, candies, and related accessories and gifts.

**Georgetown Coffee Tea and Spice** 1330 Wisconsin Avenue, N.W.; 338-3801. A delightful shop with a fine selection of coffee, tea, and spices; also gourmet kitchen supplies, gift items, and hard candies.

**M.E. Swing Co., Inc.** 1013 E Street, N.W. (downtown); 628-7601. Coffees, teas, and related equipment. Since 1916.

# CINEMA

See MOVIE THEATERS.

# CLIMATE

See WEATHER.

# CLOTHING

See CHILDREN AND CHILDREN'S THINGS; DEPARTMENT STORES; HABERDASHERIES AND TAILORS; SECONDHAND CLOTHING AND THRIFT SHOPS; SHOPPING MALLS AND CENTERS; WOMEN'S WEAR.

# CONCERTS AND CONCERT HALLS

See MUSIC.

# CONVENTION CENTER

**Washington, D.C. Convention Center** 900 9th Street, N.W. (at H Street); 789-1600. Event information: 371-4200. The eighth largest convention facility in North America is located in the heart of downtown Washington. Featuring 4 large exhibition halls and 40 meeting rooms, the ultramodern Center showcases a variety of trade shows, conventions, and public gate shows. Gallery Place and Metro Center Metro stops. Limited parking.

# COOKING UTENSILS
See HOME AND KITCHEN FURNISHINGS.

# CRAFT SHOPS AND GALLERIES

**American Hand** 2906 M Street, N.W. (Georgetown); 965-3273. Fine selection of pottery, porcelain, glass, and handcrafted jewelry in a broad price range; museum-quality pieces also.
**Appalachian Spring** 1415 Wisconsin Avenue, N.W. (Georgetown); 337-5780. Sophisticated wood pieces; also toys, quilts, quilted wear, jewelry, pottery, glass, pewter, rugs, pillows, etc. handcrafted in the United States.
**Jackie Chalkley** Foxhall Square, 3301 New Mexico Avenue, N.W. (near American University); 686-8884. Fine contemporary crafts and wearables.

See also the craft shops in the museums, such as the Museum of Modern Art of Latin America, the Textile Museum, and Renwick Gallery.

# DANCE

## Information on Performances

The *Washington Post*'s "Weekend" section, published Fridays, lists dance performances under "On Stage." See also the "Show" section on Sundays and the "Guide to the Lively Arts" appearing daily.

Washington's resident ballet company, the Washington Ballet, performs at Lisner Auditorium throughout the year. They advertise mainly in the *Washington Post*.

**District Curators** (783-0360) has information on current avant-garde dance, music, theater, and performance arts around town.

The Kennedy Center hosts world-renowned ballet and dance companies throughout the year. Events are advertised in the *Washington Post*.

Events are also published quarterly in *Calendar of Events* (see INFORMATION).

For dancing to music, see NIGHTLIFE; RESTAURANTS.

## Lessons

*Note*: Of interest may be the *Dancer's Companion, an Intermediate Guide to Getting the Most out of Dance Classes*, by Teri Loren, published by Dial Press, 1978.

**American University** Department of Performing Arts, Kreeger Music Building, Room 209, American University, Washington, D.C. 20016; 885-3420. Fall- and spring-semester courses in performance, choreography, anatomy, and arts management. Graduate and undergraduate levels. Guest artist each semester teaches technique and choreographs a performance for the students.

**Dance Place** 3225 8th Street, N.E. (2 blocks from Catholic University-Brookland Metro stop; 269-1600. Ongoing classes in modern dance and Afro-jazz.

**Danceworks** 1327 F Street, N.W.; 393-7432. Jazz, ballet, modern, and tap; all levels.

**George Washington University** Summer Dance Workshop (June), Department of Human Kinetics and Leisure Studies, 817 23rd Street, N.W., Washington, D.C. 20052; 676-6577. 34 courses are also offered during the year from beginning tap to professional classes in modern dance to choreography.

**Jones-Haywood School of Ballet** 1200 Delafield Place, N.W., Washington, D.C. 20011; 882-4039. Ballet, jazz, tap, and modern.

**Joy of Motion Dance Center** 1643 Connecticut Avenue, N.W.; 362-1320. Modern, jazz, tap, ballet, body dynamics, Afro-jazz, song and dance, repertory, styles of jazz.

**Washington School of Ballet** 3515 Wisconsin Avenue, N.W.; 362-1683. Classical ballet. Graduates are members of leading professional national and international companies, including the Washington Ballet.

Programs in dance are offered by most colleges and universities in Washington, in addition to those listed. For general information, see UNIVERSITIES.

# DAY CARE

See CHILDREN AND CHILDREN'S THINGS.

# DEPARTMENT STORES

**Garfinckel's** 14th and F Streets, N.W.; 628-7730. Boutiques at Georgetown Park (Wisconsin Avenue and M Street, N.W.); 628-8107. A women's and men's specialty store. Garfinckel's opened in 1905. Expert shopping service at the main store. Branches in the suburbs.

**Hecht's** Corner of 13th and G Streets, N.W. (Metro Center Metro stop); 628-6661. Genuine department store. Branches in the suburbs.

**Lord & Taylor** 5255 Western Avenue, N.W. (Friendship Heights Metro stop); 362-9600. Women's and men's specialty store. Branches in the suburbs.

**Neiman-Marcus** Mazza Gallerie, 5300 Wisconsin Avenue, N.W. at Western (Friendship Heights Metro stop); 966-9700. Women's and men's specialty store.

**Saks Fifth Avenue** 555 Wisconsin Avenue, Chevy Chase, Maryland; 657-9000. A women's and men's specialty store (just over the D.C. line in Maryland).

**Woodward & Lothrop** 11th and F Streets, N.W. (downtown); 347-5300. Also known as "Woodies." This is another genuine department store. Branches in the suburbs, including Chevy Chase across from Mazza Gallerie. Special services include expert alterations, fabric reweaving, drycleaning, and shoe repair and dyeing.

# DISCO

See NIGHTLIFE.

# DOCTORS

See HOSPITALS AND HEALTH EMERGENCIES.

# DRUGSTORES

The following 2 stores are open all night:

**Peoples Drug** 14th Street, N.W., and Thomas Circle (Massachusetts Avenue, downtown); 628-0720. Also, 7 Dupont Circle; 785-1466.

# EMERGENCIES

See HOSPITALS AND HEALTH EMERGENCIES.

# EXCURSIONS FROM THE CITY

These are 1-day or overnight trips. Where Gray Line Bus tours are mentioned, you may write to their Washington office at the Gray Line, 4th and E Streets, S.E., Washington, D.C. 20024 or call them at 202/479-5900. Most tours are offered March through October.

A few of the many excursions are listed here. See *One-Day Trips to Beauty and Bounty* and other guidebooks listed under BOOKS.

An excellent resource is *Washington's Attractions*, a brochure with a section on sights near Washington. Published by the Washington Convention and Visitors Association, it is available at the Tourist Information Center (see INFORMATION).

**Annapolis, Maryland** U.S. Naval Academy and Chesapeake Bay. Gray Line bus tour. This is also an easy drive from Washington (33 miles). Historic Annapolis, Inc., has information on walking tours and guided tours. Write to them at Old Treasury Building, State Circle, Annapolis, Md. 21401; 301/267-8149.

**Atlantic City** Gray Line bus tour. Gambling casinos and beaches.

**Baltimore, Maryland** Gray Line will offer a tour. Baltimore is an easy 1-hour drive from Washington. Be sure to visit Inner Harbor, where you can see HarborPlace, the World Trade Center, the National Aquarium, and many other worthwhile attractions. Write to the Baltimore Office of Promotion and Tourism, 110 W. Baltimore, Baltimore, Md. 21201, for information on walking tours, etc. The office is in the Hilton Hotel at Park Avenue (Charles Center); 301/752-8632. Hours: Monday–Friday, 9 AM–5 PM. For a recording of events, call 301/837-4630. An excellent guidebook for the downtown area is *Elizabeth Stevens' Guide to Baltimore's Inner Harbor*, published by Stemmer House, 2627 Caves Road, Owings Mills, Md. 21117. $3.50.

**Claude Moore Colonial Farm at Turkey Run** 6310 Old Georgetown Pike, McLean, Va. 22101; 703/442-7557. Twenty-five minutes into Virginia is an unusual working farm like those of the 1770s. Frequent special outdoor programs. From Washington, take the George Washington Memorial Parkway north to the Route 123 McLean exit. At the second light bear right onto Route 193; make the first right at the Claude Moore Colonial Farm sign and follow signs to visitor parking lot. Open April through December, Wednesday–Sunday, 10–4:30; on rainy days, open to scheduled groups only. Adults, $1; children under 12, 50¢.

**Colonial Williamsburg** Gray Line bus tour. Virginia's restored capital.

**Flying Circus** Bealeton, Virginia. Vintage aircraft air-shows in rural setting about 1 hour from Washington. At the end of the airshow, which begins at 2:30, you can rent a ride in one of the fabric-covered biplanes. Open Sunday late spring to early fall; ads appear in the *Washington Post*. From Washington take Route 66 west to Route 29; follow Route 29 through Warrenton to Opal, where you turn left onto Route 17 to Bealeton (this last turn is easy to miss). Watch for signs.

**Harpers Ferry and Gettysburg Battlefield** Gray Line bus tour. Rich in Civil War history.

**King's Dominion** See AMUSEMENT PARKS.

**Loudon County, Virginia** Nestled in the foothills of the Appalachian Mountains and consisting of 18th-century historical communities of Leesburg, Water-ford, Lincoln, and Middleburg, 25–30 miles west of Washington. Homes open to the public are Morven Park and Oatlands. Calendar of events and informa-tion on accommodations and dining available from Loudon County Visitor's Center, 16 West Loudon Street, Leesburg, Va. 22075; and Market Square Sta-tion, 108-B South Street, S.E., Leesburg. 703/777-0519 or from D.C. Metro area, toll free, Monday–Friday, 9–5, 478-1850; after 5 and on weekends and holidays, toll free, 478-1856.

**Mount Vernon (home of George Washington) and Old Town Alexandria, Virginia** Gray Line bus tour or Tourmobile (see TOURS). This is an easy drive from Washington. After visiting Mount Vernon, stop by Old Town Alexandria on your way back to Washington.

**Pennsylvania Dutch Country** Gray Line bus tour. Lan-caster County where the Amish live.

**Potomac Mills Mall** 2700 Potomac Mills Circle, Prince William, Va. 22192. About 40 minutes from Wash-ington is a unique shopping mall with factory outlet and off-price stores only, including IKEA Swedish fur-niture, Waccamaw Pottery, and clothing outlets. From Washington take the 14th Street Bridge into Virginia and follow signs for 395 South; continue onto 95 South to Dale City, Exit 52, and watch for signs. Mall hours Monday–Saturday, 10 AM–9:30 PM; Sunday, noon–6 PM.

**Shendandoah Valley, Virginia** Via Skyline Drive, one of the most beautiful highways in America. The northernmost town is Front Royal or Middletown, about 75 minutes west of Washington on Route 66 (take the Roosevelt Bridge). Consult the Virginia travel information office along Route 66 or write Virginia Division of Tourism, 202 North 9th Street, Richmond, Va. 23219.

**Sugar Loaf Mountain** In Comus, Maryland. An easy 1-hour drive from Washington. The climb from the parking lot to the peak is 30 minutes. There the view includes a few historical spots and as far as the Blue Ridge Mountains in Virginia. From the 495 Beltway take I-270 north toward Frederick, Maryland. Exit at Hyattstown onto Route 109 and go west 3 miles to Comus. Turn right on Comus Road and go about 2 miles to the entrance of Sugar Loaf Mountain. Open dawn to dusk daily. Admission free.

# FABRIC SHOPS

**B-Z Fabrics of Watergate, Inc.** 2560 Virginia Avenue, N.W.; 965-1616. A small shop with excellent selection of domestic and imported fabrics.

**Conran's** 3227 Grace Street, N.W. (Georgetown); 298-8300. Broad selection of contemporary fabrics for upholstery, slipcovers, and draperies.

**G Street Fabrics** 11854 Rockville Pike, Rockville, Md. 20852 (White Flint Metro stop is about a 10-minute walk to Mid-Pike Plaza at Old Georgetown Road); 301/231-8998. Mail Order Department: 231-8960. Although no longer in the city, this store is so special it is worth the visit if you want an unusually broad array of fabrics, notions, books, patterns, and services.

**Liberty of London** Georgetown Park, 3222 M Street, N.W.; 338-3711. Fabrics, ties, gifts.

# FILMS

See MOVIE THEATERS.

# GARDEN NURSERY

**Johnson's Flower Center** 40200 Wisconsin Avenue, N.W. (Tenley Mall, in back); 244-6100. Not only house and bedding plants, but shrubs, trees, and cut flowers by wire. Open daily.

**Washington National Cathedral Greenhouse** On the Cathedral grounds, Massachusetts and Wisconsin Avenues, N.W.; 537-6263. Christmas decorations, Advent wreaths, good selection of herbs, annual and perennial flowers during spring and summer, and houseplants. Monday–Saturday, 9–5, and Sunday, 10–5.

# GAY SCENE

The *Washington Blade*, the gay weekly of the nation's capital, is the best source of information you will find. Therein are "Out and About," which lists events in the gay community, "Community Notes," classified ads, and "D.C. Bar Guide." It is published Fridays and is available by subscription or at many establishments listed below. The address is 930 F Street, N.W., Suite 315, Washington, D.C. 20004; 347-2038.

## Bars/Clubs/Restaurants

Most of the establishments listed open late in the day and close in the early morning hours.

### Capitol Hill/Southeast

**Equus** 639 Pennsylvania Avenue, S.E.; 543-3113. Mostly men; restaurant; country/western.

**Mr. Henry's Restaurant** 601 Pennsylvania Avenue, S.E.; 546-8412. Jukebox to play, and live entertainment upstairs.

**The Other Side** 1345 Half Street, S.E.; 554-5141. Popular with gay women. Restaurant; drag shows on Sunday nights beginning at 10 PM; dancing.

**Phase 1** 525 8th Street, S.E.; 544-6831. A bar patronized mainly by gay women. Dancing. Identified outside by two yellow lights.

**Tracks** 1111 1st Street, S.E.; 488-3320. Video and disco bar attracting a mixed crowd. Large dance floor and all-night volleyball game every night.

## Southwest

**Lost & Found** 56 L Street, S.E.; 488-1200. Mostly men are attracted to this discreet super disco club, bar, restaurant with outdoor deck and game room.

## Downtown

**D.C. Eagle** 908 7th Street, N.W.; 347-6025. Mostly men; restaurant; happy hour; leather/Levi's/cycle.

## Dupont Circle/P Street, N.W. (Dupont Circle Metro Stop)

**Badlands** 1415 22nd Street, N.W.; 296-0505. Very popular high-tech disco. Open Thursday–Sunday. Mostly men.

**Badlands Annex** 1413 22nd Street, N.W.; 296-0505. Western-style with videos and pool table. Mostly men.

**Fraternity House** 2122 P Street, N.W. (rear entrance); 223-4917. Disco and 2 cruise bars, one with a western aura (Levi's, country/western music, pool table). Mostly men.

**Friends** 2122 P Street, N.W.; 822-8909. Piano bar equipped with a Steinway grand. Mixed crowd but mostly men. See also **Ribs and More**.

**Mr. P's** 2147 P Street, N.W.; 293-1064. A wide-screen video bar with cocktail lounge and outside patio. Levi's/casual; attracting mostly men.

**Rascal's** 1520 Connecticut Avenue, N.W.; 234-0975. Cruise bar, games, and music videos on first floor, and dining room and bar on mezzanine and top floor. This is a very popular place. Opens Saturday and Sunday at noon. Mostly men.

**Ribs and More** 2122 P Street, N.W.; 822-8909. Serving a variety of ribs, steak, etc. Nightly, 6–11.

# Bookstores

**Lambda Rising Bookstore** 1625 Connecticut Avenue, N.W., Washington, D.C. 20009; 462-6969. The best in gay and lesbian reading. Also used books and rare and out-of-print titles, record albums, greeting cards, and gifts. Daily, 10–midnight. One block north of Dupont Circle Metro stop.

# Chief Neighborhoods

**Dupont Circle** Connecticut and Massachusetts Avenues, N.W.
**Mt. Pleasant** In the vicinity of Park Road, N.W., 19th Street, 16th Street, and Shepherd Street, N.W.
**Southwest Waterfront** In the vicinity of Maine Avenue and M Street, S.W. and 4th Street, S.W. (Arena Stage area).

# Counseling/Hotlines

Gay Hotline, 833-3234.
Gay Information and Assistance, 363-3881.
Planned Parenthood of Metropolitan Washington, Men's Center, 1108 16th Street, N.W.; 347-8500.
Rape Crisis Center, 2201 P Street, N.W.; 232-0202. Hotline, 333-7273.
Washington Free Clinic, St. Stephen's Church, 16th and Newston Streets, N.W.; 667-1106. Tuesday, Thursday, 6 PM–10 PM.
Whitman-Walker Clinic, 2335 18th Street, N.W.; 332-5295.
These hotlines are located at the Whitman-Walker Clinic:
AIDS Information Hotline, 332-2437.
Lesbian Resource and Counseling Center, 332-5935.

# Events

Publicized in the *Washington Blade*:

**Gay and Lesbian Pride Day** Annual summer event organized by the P Street Festival. Held mid-June on Father's Day with a parade beginning on 16th Street, N.W., at Meridian Hill Park, winding through Columbia Road, Dupont Circle, and ending at P Street Beach for a 6-hour celebration. Extremely popular event.
**Holiday Bazaar** Organized by the P Street Festival and held during December.

## Social Groups

For a comprehensive list of the many social groups in and around Washington, see "Out and About" in the Washington Blade.

**Bet Mishpachah** Gay Synagogue of Washington, 833-1638.

**Dignity** (Gay Catholics), 332-2424.

# GENEALOGY

See LIBRARIES.

# GOURMET FOODS AND MARKETS

**Ambrosia** 5300 Wisconsin Avenue, N.W. (Friendship Heights Metro stop, Mazza Gallerie exit); 362-0677. Packaged gourmet imported and domestic food items.

**Cannon Sea Food, Inc.** 1065 31st Street, N.W. (Georgetown); 337-8366. The freshest seafood and wide selection.

**Eastern Market** 400 E. Capitol Street, N.W. (Capitol Hill). Vendors selling meat, fish, poultry, fruits, vegetables, cheese, pastries, etc. Closed Monday.

**French Market** 1632 Wisconsin Avenue, N.W. (Georgetown); 338-4828. *Boucherie, charcuterie, epicerie français.* Closed Wednesdays at 1:30, and Sundays.

**Georgetown Market** 3206 Grace Street, N.W. (west of M Street next to the Canal Towpath). In this market is a *boucherie* specializing in French cuts of meat, a greengrocers, a *cheeserie*, a poultry vendor, etc.

**Larimer's Market** 1727 Connecticut Avenue, N.W.; 332-1766. Imported and fancy foods. Delivery service.

**Margruder's Grocers** 5626 Connecticut Avenue, N.W. (near Maryland line); 244-7800. Imported and fancy foods. Here you will also find your dozen eggs and gallon of milk.

**Neam's Market, Inc.** 3217 P Street, N.W. (Georgetown); 338-4694. Fancy groceries. Delivery service.
**Sutton Place Gourmet** 3201 New Mexico Avenue, N.W.; 363-5800. Posh. Gourmet dinners to take out, too.
*Note*: **Washington Grocery Service** is a District supermarket delivery service. Give your order over the phone Monday–Saturday, 9 AM to 1 PM, and your order will be filled the same day. Shopping done at major area food chains; also at liquor and some specialty stores for clients' convenience. Payment in cash or check. Fee charged based on cost of items purchased.

# Ethnic Groceries and Delicatessens

**Acropolis Food Market, Inc.** 1206 Underwood Street, N.W. (off Georgia Avenue); 829-1414. Greek and Middle Eastern foods. Open daily; closed major holidays and Greek Easter.
**Chinatown Market** 521 H Street, N.W.; 842-0130.
**Deutsche Delicatessen and Cafe Mozart** 1331 H Street, N.W.; 347-5732. A German and Viennese deli and carryout stocked with the best sausages in town. At Christmas and Easter you can find unusual molded chocolates too. Also see listing of Cafe Mozart under RESTAURANTS.
**El Gavilan Groceries** 1646 Columbia Road, N.W.; 234-9260. Latin American and African products.
**Mangialardo & Sons, Inc.** 1317 Pennsylvania Avenue, S.E.; 543-6212. Italian and imported groceries.
**Mikado Grocery** 4709 Wisconsin Avenue, N.W.; 362-7700. Japanese products. Closed Monday.
**Posin's Bakery-Delicatessen** 5756 Georgia Avenue, N.W.; 723-7474 or 726-4424. Full line of kosher baked goods and deli items, grocery foods, carryout sandwiches, and platters.
**Skendaris Greek Imports** 1612 20th Street, N.W.; 265-9664. Greek, Middle Eastern, and Mediterranean grocery foods, deli, carryout, and gifts. Catering for small parties. Also Zorba's Cafe; see listing under RESTAURANTS.

**Vace Italian Delicatessen & Homemade Pasta** 3510 Connecticut Avenue, N.W.; 363-1999. The *freshest* pastas, meats, oils, tomatoes, and nice variety of cheeses.

**Wang's Co.** 800 7th Street, N.W.; 842-0447. Specialist in Oriental foods; also books, gifts, records, fine china, art, and jade.

See also CHEESE SHOPS; CHOCOLATE AND CANDY; COFFEE AND TEA; SHOPPING MALLS AND CENTERS.

# GYMS/INDOOR SPORTS FACILITIES/ HOT TUBS

**Making Waves** 1213 Bank Street, N.W. (Georgetown); 337-8827. Private room, tub, shower, lighting, music; towels supplied. Open Sunday–Thursday, 11 AM–midnight; Friday and Saturday, 11 AM–2 AM. Call for rates.

**Office Health Center** 1990 M Street, N.W. (downtown); 872-0222. Treadmills, resistive weight equipment (including Nautilus and Life Cycle), whirlpools, steam rooms, sauna, coed aerobic classes, lockers, and showers. Men's facilities completely separate from women's facilities. Daily, weekly, and monthly rates available. Monday–Friday, 7:30 AM–9 PM; Saturday, 11–6; closed Sunday.

**YMCA** 1711 Rhode Island Avenue, N.W. (Dupont Circle); 862-9622. Swimming pool; banked running track; squash, handball and racquetball courts; gym; Nautilus room; Universal Super Circuit room; exercise and weight room; sauna and steam room; whirlpool; lamp room; nap room; and lounge. Special guest fee if you are a member of the YMCA elsewhere.

**YWCA** 624 9th Street, N.W. (downtown); 638-2100. Swimming pool, gymnasium, and volleyball, basketball, slimnastics, tiny tots gym, aerobics classes.

# HABERDASHERIES AND TAILORS

**Arduino D'Orazio Custom Tailor Shop and Tuxedo Rental Shop** 2600 Connecticut Avenue, N.W. (entrance on Calvert Street); 265-3742. "Tailor to the top threaders."

**Arthur A. Adler, Inc.** 1101 Connecticut Avenue, N.W. in the Connecticut Connection (downtown); 628-0131. Traditional menswear and furnishings, shoes, Southwick clothing. Farragut North Metro stop.

**Britches of Georgetown** 1247 Wisconsin Avenue, N.W.; 338-3330. Also at 1219 Connecticut Avenue, N.W. (downtown); 347-8994. Classic and designer menswear, sportswear, furnishings, and shoes.

**Brooks Brothers** 1840 L Street, N.W. (downtown); 659-4650. Traditional menswear, furnishings, and shoes. Also departments for young men, boys, and women. Farragut North Metro stop.

**Dash's Designers** 111 19th Street, N.W. (downtown); 296-4470. Also at 1309 F Street, N.W. (downtown); 737-6009; and at 3229 M Street, N.W. (Georgetown); 338-4050. Discounts from the world's leading fashion designers for men.

**Georgetown University Shop** 1248 36th Street, N.W.; 337-8100. Burberry's English raincoats, authentic Irish walking hats, classic clothing, furnishings, and shoes. Women's apparel also.

**Jos. A Bank Clothiers** 1118 19th Street, N.W. (downtown); 466-2282. Traditional and classic clothing at discount. Women's apparel also. Farragut North Metro stop.

**Raleighs** 1133 Connecticut Avenue, N.W. (downtown); 785-7071. Also at Mazza Gallerie, Wisconsin and Western Avenues, N.W. (uptown); 785-7011. Hart Schaffner & Marx, Hickey-Freeman, furnishings and shoes. Women's apparel also.

**Ralph Lauren-Polo Shop** 1220 Connecticut Avenue, N.W. (downtown); 463-7460. Designer suits, sportswear, and furnishings. Women's apparel also.

# HANDICAPPED INDIVIDUALS' RESOURCES

**D.C. Center for Independent Living** 1400 Florida Avenue, N.E.; 388-0033. This organization responds quickly to the need of the handicapped visitor, whether it is locating emergency attendant care or telling you who can repair your wheelchair. They will help make your visit to Washington worry-free and enjoyable.

**Information Center for Handicapped Individuals** 605 G Street, N.W., Suite 202A, Washington, D.C. 20001; 347-4986 or TTY, 347-8320. Located downtown at 6th and G Streets. Information, referral, protection, and advocacy services; Spanish-speaking and signing staff. When ordering publications by mail, include payment by check or money order. Publications are also available at the Center Monday–Friday, 9–5. Publications recommended:

*Access Washington: A Guide to Metropolitan D.C. for the Physically Handicapped.* Very detailed information on the accessibility of aisles, approaches, entrances, designated seating and parking, water fountains, restrooms, Braille, etc., in a set of 6 brochures. Brochure titles are (1) "Theater & Stage, Sights of Interest"; (2) "Hotels/Motels"; (3) "Stadiums, Auditoriums, Recreation"; (4) "Malls & Department Stores, Museums & Galleries, Libraries"; (5) Restaurants"; and (6) "Thought You'd Like to Know" (information on available support services). Published 1986. $3.75 + 63¢ postage ($4.38) for the set of 6 brochures, or 75¢ + 22¢ postage for individual brochures.

*Directory of Services for Handicapping Conditions.* Lists all services available in the Metropolitan area. Identifies services that have bilingual staff and TTY. Published 1986 and available by mail.

*Here Comes the Sun.* Summarizes all summer programs for handicapped children in Metropolitan D.C. Published every May. $3 + 63¢ postage.

**Smithsonian Institution** From the Smithsonian, *A Guide for Disabled Visitors*. Available at any information desk. Visitors may also request information by calling 357-2700 (voice) or 357-1729 (TDD) between 9 AM and 5 PM daily (except Christmas Day). For more specific information on programs of special interest for disabled visitors, call 357-1697 (voice) or 357-1691 (TDD).

**Theater Audio Service of the Washington Ear** Provides experienced volunteer commentators for certain performances at Arena Stage, Kennedy Center, and National Theatre through a Phonic Ear, which must be reserved at the box office. This service is free.

**Washington Ear, Inc.** 35 University Boulevard East, Silver Spring, Md. 20901; 681-6636. Free closed-circuit radio reading service broadcast over a subcarrier channel of WETA-FM. The *Washington Post, Wall Street Journal*, and magazines and books are read every day. A large-print map of Washington, D.C., sells for $5; in Braille, $12. (Similar map of Maryland also available.) Cassettes about interesting aspects of Washington are available at $8.50/cassette or $35 for 6 cassettes which include all 11 programs on Washington. Orders must include payment; price includes postage.

*Special services* for the blind, deaf, and hard-of-hearing are available at many theaters. The patron requiring these is reminded to inquire about them at the time he or she purchases tickets. Tickets are often reduced in price for the handicapped patron, and the special services are usually free.

See also TRANSPORTATION.

# HEALTH CARE
See HOSPITALS AND HEALTH EMERGENCIES.

# HEALTH CLUBS
See GYMS/INDOOR SPORTS FACILITIES/HOT TUBS.

# HOBBY SHOPS

Washington is sorely in need of fine hobby shops; downtown redevelopment sent the few businesses there were to the suburbs. The best one in the suburbs for serious modelers is:

**Squadron Shop** 12351-A Georgia Avenue, Glenmont, Md.; 942-7410 or 942-7427. Plastic airplane, ship, and car kits; military modeling, war games, books, and extensive selection of decals. Tuesday–Saturday, 10 AM–9 PM; Sunday, 12–6 PM.

At least there is still a shop for trains in the District:

**Downtown Lock & Electric Co.** 1324 14th Street, N.W. (between Rhode Island Avenue and N Street); 265-5990. Lionel distributor since 1910. Sells and services new and old models. Monday–Saturday, 9:30 AM–2:30 PM. During weekends in December prior to Christmas, Saturday hours are extended and the shop is open Sunday.

# HOLIDAYS
See ANNUAL EVENTS.

# HOME AND KITCHEN FURNISHINGS

**Conran's** 3227 Grace Street, N.W. (Georgetown); 298-8300. European home furnishings, furniture, housewares, lighting, linens, rugs, accessories, and fabrics.

**Door Store** 3140 M Street, N.W. (Georgetown); 333-7737. Contemporary furniture and accessories.

**Kitchen Bazaar** 4455 Connecticut Avenue, N.W. (at Yuma Street); 244-1550. Complete selection of international cookware and serving accessories.

**Laura Ashley** 3213 M Street, N.W. (Georgetown); 338-5481. Such items as bed linens, lamps, tiles, fabric, wallpaper, and related accessories for the home bear the Laura Ashley trademarks: romantic, Victorian, small, country prints; nostalgic patterns of the '20s, '30s, '40s, and '50s; and suave, sophisticated elegant designs.

**Little Caledonia Shop** 1419 Wisconsin Avenue, N.W. (Georgetown); 333-4700. Fine collection of domestic and imported gifts, kitchenware, glassware, and fabrics in the traditional style. Greeting cards, toys, and, in season, a wonderful array of Christmas decorations.

**Martin's of Georgetown** 1304 Wisconsin Avenue, N.W.; 338-6144. Washington's largest selection of dinnerware and giftware, and a few antiques.

**Midnight Sun Design Centre** 1700 Pennsylvania Avenue, N.W.; 393-4769. Fine contemporary Scandinavian accessories and gifts.

**Roche Bobois** 4200 Wisconsin Avenue, N.W. (uptown); 966-4490. Contemporary furniture. Closed weekends.

**Scan** 3222 M Street, N.W. (Georgetown Park Mall); 333-5015. Contemporary furniture and accessories.

**Theodore's** 2233 Wisconsin Avenue, N.W. (N. Georgetown); 333-2300. Contemporary furniture and accessories.

**Uzzolo** 3222 M Street, N.W.; 342-1551. Also at 1718 Connecticut Avenue, N.W.; 328-0900. High-tech and sophisticated Italian linens and gifts. Furniture at Connecticut Avenue store.

**W. Bell & Co., Inc.** 1901 L Street, N.W. Also at 1220 Wisconsin Avenue, N.W.; 881-2000. Household merchandise, jewelry, and photographic equipment at discounted prices. Branches in the suburbs.

**W & J Sloane** 1130 Connecticut Avenue, N.W. (downtown); 659-9200. Traditional and contemporary furniture and rugs.

**Washington Design Center** 300 D Street, S.W.; 554-5053. This center, sheathed in glass, has over 200 furniture and accessory showrooms. Admission limited to design professionals and their clients. Atop the Federal Center Metro stop.

**Williams-Sonoma** at Mazza Gallerie, 5300 Wisconsin Avenue, N.W.; 244-4800. Hard-to-find items, professional cooking equipment and accessories.

See also DEPARTMENT STORES.

# HOSPITALS AND HEALTH EMERGENCIES

**Capitol Hill Hospital** 700 Constitution Avenue, N.E.;
269-8000. Emergency: 269-8769.
**Children's Hospital National Medical Center** 111
Michigan Avenue, N.W.; 745-5000. Emergency: 745-
5203.
**Columbia Hospital for Women Medical Center** 2425
L Street, N.W.; 293-6500. (This hospital does not have
an emergency room.)
**George Washington University Hospital** 901 23rd
Street, N.W. (downtown at Washington Circle, Foggy
Bottom Metro stop); 676-6000. Emergency: 676-3211.
**Georgetown University Hospital** 3800 Reservoir
Road, N.W.; 625-0100. Emergency: 625-7151.
**Sibley Memorial Hospital** 5255 Loughboro Road,
N.W.; 537-4000. Emergency: 537-4080.
**Washington Hospital Center** 110 Irving, N.W.; 541-
0500. Emergency: 541-6701.
**Poison Control Center** At Georgetown University
Hospital; 202/625-3333. (If you have children in your
home, you may wish to call the Center to request a
free sheet of green "Mr. Yuk" stickers to place on areas
young children should stay away from.)

# HOTELS AND MOTELS

*Washington's Accommodations*, a guide that lists rates
of hotels and motor inns in the Washington area, is
free by request from the Washington, D.C. Convention
and Visitors Association, 1575 I Street, N.W., Washington, D.C. 20005. When in town, pick up this brochure at the Tourist Information Center (see INFOR-
MATION).
*Washington, Just Waiting to be Discovered*, an up-to-
date guide to reduced weekend rates in Washington's
hotels, is published by the Hotel Association of Wash-

ington, P.O. Box 33578, Washington, D.C. 20033. The Tourist Information Center also has copies of this guide (which locates the hotels on a map).

If you are staying at a hotel with a concierge, remember to rely on his or her ability to get those dinner reservations and theater tickets when you have been told "there is nothing available." Concierges are eager to share their expertise and broad knowledge of tourist Washington.

A few of the many places to stay in Washington are listed below. These hotels have air-conditioning and garages (or garages are nearby) unless noted. Be sure to inquire about special weekend rates, New Year's Eve packages, and reduced rates for seniors, families, and corporate, government, education, and embassy officials. Rates are subject to change without notice. There is a 10% sales tax and $1 occupancy tax per room per night.

When visiting a city as exciting as Washington, many people here on business would like to bring their families with them. Child care is not as difficult to arrange as it might seem. **Sitters Unlimited** is described under CHILDREN AND CHILDREN'S THINGS—DAY CARE AND SITTING SERVICES. And note the unique program at the Hyatt Regency Washington Hotel on Capitol Hill, described below.

# Capitol Hill

**Bellevue Hotel** 15 E Street, N.W., at North Capitol Street (Union Station Metro stop), 20001; 638-0900. Collect calls will be accepted for reservations. This recently renovated, small, older hotel has 140 large rooms. Popular Tiber Creek Pub features yards of beer. Singles from $79; doubles from $91; suites from $130.

**Hyatt Regency Washington** 400 New Jersey Avenue, N.W. (Union Station or Judiciary Square Metro stops), 20001; 737-1234 or 800/228-9000. This 840-room hotel conveniently located within walking distance of Capitol Hill and the Mall, has several award-winning restaurants, including Hugo's, with a view of Capitol Hill. Inquire about the availability of the Children's Suite, an innovative service unique to the Hyatt Regency and offered for the first time during the summer of 1986. The day-care program, under the direction of the YMCA and available Monday–Sunday, 8 AM to midnight, during July and August, will be offered at other times during the year if proven successful. Other amenities include a new pool and complete fitness center. Concierge services. The Old Town Trolley begins its tours here (see TOURS). Singles from $129; doubles from $149; suites from $325. Weekend rates offered. Summer rates are $95/day/room and on weekends, $84/day/room.

**Phoenix Park Hotel** 520 North Capitol Street (Union Station Metro stop), 20001; 638-6900 or 800/824-5419. An 88-room luxury hotel within walking distance of the major attractions on Capitol Hill and not so far from the Mall. Phoenix Park is home to the Dubliner, a popular watering hole featuring Irish folk music, and to the Powerscourt, Washington's one and only elegant Irish restaurant. Concierge services. Singles from $138; doubles from $157; suites, $250–450 (3 penthouse suites). Weekend rates available.

## Southwest (Near the Mall and Waterfront)

**Loew's L'Enfant Plaza Hotel** 480 L'Enfant Plaza, S.W. (L'Enfant Plaza Metro stop), 20024; 484-1000 or 800/223-0888. 372 rooms. Luxury hotel set among large government buildings. Concierge services. Singles from $115; doubles from $135; suites from $295. Several weekend packages offered.

## Downtown

**American Youth Hostel, Potomac Area Council** At press time, the new address for the International Youth Hostel was not available. Please call the Potomac Area Council for up-to-date information: 783-4943 (see BICYCLES AND BICYCLING).

**Guest Quarters** 801 New Hampshire Avenue, N.W. (Foggy Bottom Metro stop), 20037; 785-2000 or 800/424-2900. In Foggy Bottom, near the Kennedy Center. Also at 2500 Pennsylvania Avenue, N.W., 20037; 333-8060. Guest services. Suites with fully equipped kitchen, living room, and bedroom. Single, $140; double, $160.

**Harrington Hotel** 11th and E Streets, N.W. (Metro Center Metro stop), 20004; 628-8140 or 800/424-8532. Large, rambling, 308-room hotel attracting students on school trips and families visiting the Smithsonian. Cafeteria, cocktail lounge, and sandwich shop. Free parking for cars only, with a $1 in/out charge per 24 hours. Vans may be parked 2 blocks away; the guest is reimbursed $5 for each 24-hour period. Singles from $40; doubles from $52; family (4 persons), $55; family (2 rooms together), $88. Senior citizen discounts.

**Hotel Lombardy** 2010 I Street, N.W. (Farragut West Metro stop), 20006; 828-2600 or 800/424-5486. Small, downtown, all-suite hotel with kitchens equipped to serve 4 people. Located halfway between George Washington University and the White House. Deluxe and executive suites, $70–$125; special weekend rates available.

**Hotel Washington** 15th Street and Pennsylvania Avenue, N.W. (Metro Center Metro stop), 20004; 638-5900 or 800/424-9540. Completely restored and renovated, this 350-room hotel with a quiet ambience is a centrally located Washington landmark, the cornerstone of the downtown restoration on the Inaugural Parade route. Seasonal skywalk and sidewalk cafés and rooftop dining provide sweeping views of Washington's monuments. Guest services. Singles from $99; doubles from $111; suites from $260. Special weekend rates, discount of 25%.

**J. W. Marriott Hotel** 1331 Pennsylvania Avenue, N.W. (Metro Center Metro stop), 20004; 393-2000 or 800/228-9290. This sparkling 773-room hotel is conveniently located on the Inaugural Parade route and next door to The Shops at National Place and The National, and within walking distance of the museums along the Mall. Formal dining room, family-style restaurant, lounge, and deli-bar facilities. Concierge services. Singles from $170; doubles from $190; concierge-levels available, with singles from $185 and doubles from $195. Special weekend rates and packages and senior citizen discounts for AARP members.

**One Washington Circle Hotel** One Washington Circle (Foggy Bottom Metro stop), 20037; 872-1680 or 800/424-9671. This quiet, all-suite hotel is within walking distance of the Kennedy Center and George Washington University Hospital, and 6 blocks from Georgetown, the White House, and adjacent business and financial districts. Each of the 151 suites has a fully equipped kitchen. Concierge services. Swimming pool open seasonally. Dining includes the West End Cafe with piano bar, and 2 nice restaurants. Suites from $120; double occupancy, $15 additional. Special weekend rates; also, senior citizen discounts on weekends.

**Radisson Henley Park Hotel** 926 Massachusetts Avenue, N.W. (Gallery Place or Metro Center Metro stops), 20001; 638-5200 or 800/222-8474. In this 96-room hotel, afternoon high tea is served in the Wilkes Room (daily, 4–6 PM), and live music is featured in Marley's Lounge (Monday–Saturday). The formal restaurant, Coeur de Lion, specializes in French cuisine. Concierge service and valet parking. Singles from $105; doubles from $125; suites from $200. Special weekend rates and packages.

**Westin Hotel** 2401 M Street, N.W. (Foggy Bottom Metro stop), 20037; 429-2400; for reservations, 800/228-3000. This new 416-room hotel is within walking distance of Georgetown and the Kennedy Center. It sports the Colonnade and Bistro restaurants and a Nautilus fitness center with indoor pool and squash courts. Concierge services. Singles from $145; doubles from $165; suites from $290. Children under 18 free. Special weekend rates offered subject to availability.

**Willard Inter-Continental Hotel** 1401 Pennsylvania Avenue, N.W. (Metro Center or Federal Triangle Metro stop), 20004; 628-9100. This newly restored 394-room hotel is a National Landmark known as the "Residence of Presidents." Located between Garfinckel's and the Tourist Information Center and on the Inaugural Parade route. Singles from $160; doubles from $180; suites from $350 ($2,000 for the Presidential Suite). Weekend packages offered.

# Georgetown

**Four Seasons** 2800 Pennsylvania Avenue, N.W., 20007; 342-0444 or 800/828-1188. An elegant 208-room hotel located at the edge of Georgetown and adjacent to the Canal Towpath. Great dining, afternoon tea, and disco; *Esquire* rated their bar as one of Washington's 4 best. Concierge services. Rooms from $140 to $200; suites from $300 to $1,000. Special weekend package.

**Georgetown Dutch Inn** 1075 Thomas Jefferson Street, N.W., 20007; 337-0900. A small, intimate, European-style hotel with 47 one- and two-bedroom suites with fully equipped kitchenettes. Nice restaurant and bar. Adjacent to the Canal Towpath and near Washington Harbour. Concierge services. Singles from $95; doubles from $105; penthouse from $200. Special weekend rates, singles and doubles, $85. Rates include breakfast and free parking.

**Georgetown Inn** 1310 Wisconsin Avenue, N.W., 20007; 333-8900 or 800/424-2979. Located in the heart of Georgetown, this inn has concierge service and 95 plush and deluxe rooms. The popular and well-reviewed Georgetown Bar & Grill has a raw bar and a piano bar, and serves brunch on Saturday and Sunday. Indoor and outdoor parking at the inn. Singles from $125; doubles from $140; suites from $210. Special weekend rates and packages.

## Connecticut Avenue

**Adams Inn** 1744 Lanier Place, N.W. (Woodley Park Zoo Metro stop), 20009; 745-3600. Warm, home-style inn providing bed and breakfast. Located in the vibrant Adams Morgan neighborhood. Some rooms with private bath. Limited garages available at $3/night. Rates from $30 to $55.

**Carlyle Suites** 1731 New Hampshire Avenue, N.W. (Dupont Circle Metro stop, Q Street exit), 20009; 234-3200. This is an all-suite hotel recently renovated in the Art Deco style. Each of the 175 suites has an equipped kitchen. Home of Jimmy K's restaurant. Singles from $59; doubles from $69. Special weekend rates.

**The Dolley Madison Hotel** 1507 M Street, N.W. (Farragut North or McPherson Square Metro stops), 20005; 862-1600 or 800/424-8577. Luxury 42-room bed-and-breakfast hotel. Patrons are welcome to the amenities available at the Madison Hotel across the street. Including a continental breakfast, singles from $125; doubles from $145; suites from $180.

**Farragut West** 1808 I Street, N.W. (across street from Farragut West Metro stop), 20006; 393-2400. Quaint 76-room hotel conveniently located near Market Square and Sholl's cafeteria. Single, $44; double, $54;

triple, $64; 2 adjoining rooms sleeping 4, $74; suites, $84. Weekend rates available. Ten percent discount for senior citizens and students, government and military employees.

**Gralyn** 1745 N Street, N.W. (Dupont Circle Metro stop), 20036; 785-1515. This very accommodating, small, quiet, English-style 35-room inn was formerly the Persian Embassy, a group of converted townhouses built *c.* 1880. A full, hearty breakfast is served for $3.25, which may be enjoyed in the Victorian garden, weather permitting. The management provides trays if guests wish to picnic in the garden at other times. Rooms with bath have air-conditioning; rooms with shared bath have fans. Free parking in back of hotel. Singles w/shared bath from $35; singles w/bath from $50; doubles from $60; apartments from $50. Family rates available.

**Madison Hotel** 15th and M Streets, N.W. (McPherson Square Metro stop), 20005; 862-1600 or 800/424-8577. One of the finest hotels in Washington, with an excellent restaurant, the Montpelier Room. 365 rooms. Concierge services. Singles from $135; doubles from $160; suites from $290.

**Mayflower** 1127 Connecticut Avenue, N.W. (Farragut North Metro stop), 20036; 347-3000 or 800/HOTELS-1. The Mayflower, a Stouffer hotel and a National Landmark, is a 724-room traditional hotel in the European manner. Cafe Promenade features New American cuisine, and the restored Town & Country restaurant is a favorite of the local and political crowd. Concierge services. Singles from $135 and doubles from $245. Special weekend rates (50% off), and packages based on availability.

**Normandy Inn** 2118 Wyoming Avenue, N.W. (Dupont Circle Metro stop), 20008; 483-1350 or 800/424-3729. Small, charming, 74-room hotel on the corner of Connecticut Avenue. Some rooms with small refrigerators. Continental breakfast served; restaurants nearby. Complimentary tea and coffee from 11 AM to midnight, and cookies in the afternoon. Singles, $70; doubles, $80. Special weekend rates, $50/night single or double including continental breakfast and a bottle of wine.

**Tabard Inn** 1739 N Street, N.W. (Dupont Circle Metro stop), 20036; 785-1277. Small, charming and romantic

40-room inn with excellent dining room and bar. *Esquire* rated the bar one of Washington's 4 best. Patio used for breakfast and lunch, weather permitting. Make reservations well in advance. Single w/shared bath from $43; double w/shared bath from $60; single with private bath from $70; double with private bath from $85; each extra person, $15. Includes continental breakfast. Visa and MasterCard are the only cards accepted.

**Vista International Hotel** 1400 M Street, N.W. (McPherson Square Metro stop), 20005; 429-1700 or 800/VISTA-DC (800/847-8232). In this 400-room hotel are a fitness center, the well-reviewed formal American Harvest Restaurant, the Veranda restaurant in the atrium, and the Lobby Court Cafe, which serves a light afternoon tea. Concierge services. Singles from $130; doubles from $150; suites from $220. Special weekend packages.

**Washington Hilton** 1919 Connecticut Avenue, N.W. (Dupont Circle Metro stop), 20009; 483-3000 or 800/HIL-TONS. This is Washington's largest in-town "resort" with 1,150 rooms, health club, tennis court, Jacuzzi, and other indoor and outdoor recreational facilities. Tower accommodations with special amenities and facilities available. This Hilton has the city's largest ballroom, 32 meeting rooms, an exhibit hall, and a permanent video teleconferencing room. Concierge services. Singles from $85; doubles from $105; suites from $240. Special weekend rates and packages.

Look under Motels in the D.C. Yellow Pages for a complete list of hotels and motels in the Washington area. The AAA *Mid-Atlantic Tour Book* or your travel agent would also be of help if you prefer to stay in the suburbs near public transportation. Motels along Wilson Boulevard in Arlington, Virginia, are within walking distance of restaurants and Metrorail.

# ICE CREAM

**Baskin Robbins** 1823 L Street, N.W., 296-3131. Also at 5502 Connecticut Avenue, N.W. near Chevy Chase

Circle at the Maryland line, 966-1908. Thirty-one flavors.

**Bob's Famous Homemade Ice Cream** 2416 Wisconsin Avenue, N.W. (Georgetown just below Calvert Street); 965-4499.

**Haagen-Dazs Ice Cream Shop** 1524 Connecticut Avenue, N.W. (Dupont Circle); 667-0350. Also at 1438 Wisconsin Avenue, N.W. (Georgetown); 333-7505, and at 205 Pennsylvania Avenue, S.E. (Capitol Hill); 543-0605.

**Ice Cream Lobby** 615 Pennsylvania Avenue, S.E. (Capitol Hill); 547-3279. This is a nice cafe serving light foods and cappucino. On exhibit is the work of local young professional artists.

**Swensen's Ice Cream** 3414 Connecticut Avenue, N.W.; 362-3590. Also in Esplanade Mall on the corner of 20th and I Streets, N.W.; 833-1140. In Georgetown at 1254 Wisconsin Avenue, N.W.; 333-3433. At Mazza Gallerie, 5310 Wisconsin Avenue, N.W.; 966-8606. In Tenley Mall at 4200 Wisconsin Avenue, N.W.; 244-5544. Serving sandwiches and freshly made ice cream delights.

**Thomas Sweet** 3214 P Street, N.W.; 337-0616. Imaginative ice cream parlor specializing in gourmet flavors blended with your choice of fruit and candies. Creative homemade molded chocolates and cookies. Monday–Sunday early noon 'til very late or wee hours weekends.

# INFORMATION

## Emergency Telephone Numbers

Ambulance Emergency: 911.
Deaf Emergency: 727-9334.
Fire Emergency: 911.
Police Emergency: 911.
U.S. Park Police Emergency: 426-6600.

Alcohol and Drug Hotline: 727-0474.
Crime Solvers and Tipsters Confidential Phone: 393-2222.

Crisis Line: 561-7000.
Family & Children in Trouble (FACT) Hotline: 628-3228.
Mayor's Command Center, 24-hour assistance for D.C. residents: 727-6161.
Missing and Exploited Children Hotline: from Washington D.C. telephones, dial 634-9836; from all other telephones, including those in Virginia and Maryland, dial 800/843-5678.
Poison Control Center: 625-3333.
Rape Crisis Hotline: 333-R-A-P-E (333-7273) or the Rape Crisis Center: 232-0202.
Traffic Control, Car Towed: 727-5000.
VD Hotline: 832-7000.

## Helpful Telephone Numbers

Area Code for D.C.: 202 (for Maryland: 301; for Virginia: 703 and 804).

Time: 844-2525 (Eastern Standard Time).
Weather: 936-1212.
Washington Convention and Visitors Association: 789-7000.
WCVA's Dial-an-Event: 737-8866.
Handicapped Individuals Information: 347-4986; TDD: 347-8320. See also HANDICAPPED INDIVIDUALS' RESOURCES.
Lost & Found: If you have lost something in a taxi, the nearest police precinct will keep things. If you remember the name, number, or fleet of your taxi driver, call 727-5401. If you have lost something in the subway or on a bus, call 637-1195.
Metrorail and Metrobus Information: 637-7000 (6 AM–11:30 PM).
Metrorail and Metrobus Information, TDD: 638-3780. See also TRANSPORTATION.
Passport Office: 783-8200.
Smithsonian Information: 357-2700.
Visa Information, Alien Only: 663-1972.

## Other Useful Telephone Numbers

Children's Story: 638-5717.
Congressional offices, committees, and subcommittees: 224-3121.

Dental Referral Service of the D.C. Dental Society: 686-0803.

Dial-a-Park: 426-6975 (for special events information: 426-6690).

Dial-a-Phenomenon Smithsonian Institution: 357-2000.

Dial-a-Museum Smithsonian Institution: 357-2020.

Lawyer Referral Service of the D.C. Bar Assoc.: 331-4365.

Physicians Referral Service of the Medical Society of D.C.: 466-1880.

Planned Parenthood: 347-8500.

Sports Scores: 223-8060.

# Information for Visitors

**Tourist Information Center** Great Hall, U.S. Commerce Department, 14th Street and Pennsylvania Avenue, N.W.; 789-7000. One block from the White House. Operated by the Washington Convention and Visitors Association with assistance by volunteers from the International Visitors Information Service and Travelers Aid. Upon entering, tourists will find an information desk full of brochures about the local hotels, restaurants, transportation and tour companies, and leisure activities. Booths also maintained by the National Park Service and White House Historical Association. Monday–Friday, 9–5 PM. Also Saturday–Sunday, 9–5, April through October. Weekend hours determined annually.

**Washington Convention and Visitors Association** 1575 I Street, N.W.; 20005; 789-7000. Dial-an-Event: 737-8866. Information published for the domestic and international visitor. Free brochures include *Washington's Attractions*, listing cultural and other events every season (the most complete listing available in advance); *Dining/Shopping Guide*, offering the best of both worlds; *Washington's Accommodations*, listing hotels and rates in the metropolitan area; and the *Washington Visitor Map*. The visitor is encouraged to visit the Tourist Information Center at 14th Street and Pennsylvania Avenue, N.W., in the Great Hall of the Department of Commerce. These brochures are only a few among the wide variety you will find at the Center (see **Tourist Information Center**, above) OR

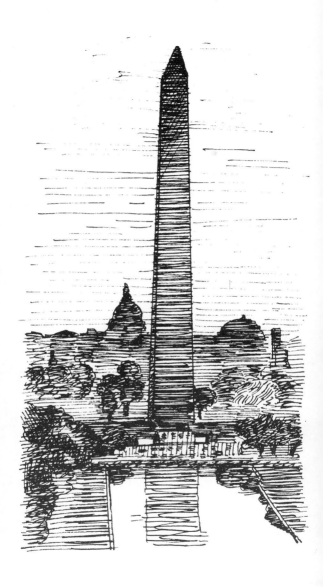

WASHINGTON MONUMENT

you may request these by mail at the above address. McPherson Square Metro stop.

**International Visitors Information Service (IVIS)** 733 15th Street, N.W., Suite 300, Washington, D.C., 20005; 783-6540. Monday–Friday, 9 AM–5 PM. Reception centers also at Dulles International Airport daily, noon to 7 PM, and at the Tourist Information Center, 14th Street and Pennsylvania Avenue, N.W. (see **Tourist Information Center**, above). Complete travel and sightseeing information for the foreign tourist in English and other languages.

**Exchanging foreign currency** can be accomplished at Dulles International Airport, Baltimore International Airport, or at many banks and hotels in downtown Washington. In the business of foreign currency is:

**Deak-Perera Washington** 1800 K Street, N.W. (downtown at 18th Street); 872-1233. Weekdays, 9–5. Farragut West Metro stop.

# Preparing for Your Visit to Washington

**Smithsonian** visitors are encouraged to request a "previsit packet" *in advance* of their trip by writing or calling Visitor Information and Associates' Reception Center, Smithsonian Institution, Washington, D.C. 20560 (357-2700).

**Publications** such as *Museum Washington*, the *Washingtonian*, and the *Washington Post* (see NEWSPAPERS AND MAGAZINES), in addition to the brochures available free of charge from the Washington Convention and Visitors Association (see above), are worthwhile sources of up-to-date information on events in the city.

# Calendars of Events

Available by mail or at the various galleries and institutions. To receive a calendar each month, call or write and request to be placed on the calendar of events mailing list. These calendars not only keep you up to date on exhibitions but also list concerts, lectures, films, new publications, tours, demonstrations, etc. Free unless noted.

**Calendar of Events** Published quarterly by the Washington Convention and Visitors Association, 1575

I Street, N.W., Washington, D.C. 20005; 789-7000. Available free from the Tourist Information Center. Lists cultural and special events of interest each season. The most complete list of these activities in advance.

**Corcoran Gallery of Art** 17th Street and New York Avenue, N.W., Washington, D.C. 20006; 638-3211. Sent to members.

**D.C. Department of Recreation** 3149 16th Street, N.W., Washington, D.C. 20010. "Do You Know," $4/year; for a single complimentary copy, send a self-addressed stamped envelope.

**Folger Shakespeare Library** 201 E. Capitol Street, S.E., Washington, D.C. 20003; 544-7077.

**Hirshhorn Museum & Sculpture Garden** Washington, D.C. 20560; 357-1618. Lists marvelous Saturday-morning films for children.

**Kiosk** Published by National Capitol Region of the National Park Service. Office of Public Affairs, 1100 Ohio Drive, S.W., Washington, D.C. 20242. "Kiosk" is also available at the Jefferson, Lincoln, and Washington Monuments or at the kiosk on the Ellipse.

**Library of Congress** Central Services Division, Printing & Processing Section, Washington, D.C. 20540; 287-5588.

**National Air and Space Museum** Washington, D.C. 20560; 357-1552.

**National Archives and Record Service** Room G-6, Washington, D.C. 20408; 523-3099. Includes seminars on genealogical research.

**National Gallery of Art** Washington, D.C. 20565; 842-6043.

**National Museum of American Art and the Phillips Collection** 1600 21st Street, N.W., Washington, D.C. 20009; 387-2151.

**Renwick Gallery** Smithsonian Institution, Washington, D.C. 20560; 357-2247.

**Smithsonian Institution** Only available in the newspaper, usually published the last Friday of the month (sometimes the next-to-the-last Friday of the month) in the "Weekend" section of the *Washington Post*. This calendar lists a representative selection of events at the individual museums. For a comprehensive list of events at the individual museums, consult the calendar of events published by that museum.

**Washington National Cathedral** Wisconsin and Massachusetts Avenues, N.W., Washington, D.C. 20016. Communications Office, 537-6200. Complimentary copy; subscription, $5/year.

## Radio & TV Stations

**WAMU-88.5 FM** (noncommercial) Weekdays, talk in the morning, bluegrass in the afternoon, "All Things Considered" at 6:30, talk in the evening, jazz through the night. Weekends, bluegrass, jazz, "All Things Considered," and vintage radio. (For a complimentary copy of the monthly program guide, call 885-1030.)

**WETA-90.9 FM** (noncommercial) Mainly classical; live transmission of "Prairie Home Companion" (Saturdays at 6 PM, repeated on Sundays at 1 PM), important hearings on Capitol Hill, and National Press Club luncheon guests' speeches, etc.; "All Things Considered" at 5 PM. Some orchestra and opera programs are simulcast with WETA Channel 26 television. 998-2790.

**WGMS-570 AM and 103.5 FM** Classical music and news. 468-1800.

**WMAL-630 AM** Washington favorite in the morning, with Hardin and Weaver. 686-3100.

**WPFW-89.3 FM** (noncommercial) A Pacifica Radio station; jazz and talk. Children's story hour on Saturdays, 8–9 AM, with listener call-in feature. 783-3100.

**WRC-980 AM** Talk, listener call-in, news, sports. 587-4900.

**WTOP-1500 AM** News, weather, traffic, and sports information. Larry King show weeknights, 11 PM; weekends, 12:05 AM. 364-5800.

**ABC: Channel 7, WJLA**
**CBS: Channel 9, WDVM**
**NBC: Channel 4, WRC**
**PBS: Channel 26 (UHF), WETA** (noncommercial) Children's shows, "MacNeil-Lehrer," "Nightly Business Report," "Washington Week in Review," "Sneak Previews," "Wall Street Week," etc. Some orchestra and opera programs are simulcast with WETA radio.

**PBS: Channel 32 (UHF), WHMM** (noncommercial) Similar programming to other PBS stations, including "Wonderworks," "Newton's Apple," "Wall Street Week," "Mystery!" and "3-2-1 Contact."

**PBS: Channel 22 (UHF), WMPT** (noncommercial) Similar programming to other PBS stations, including "Masterpiece Theater," "Agronsky & Company," "Sesame Street," and "Lassie."

Other radio and television stations are listed daily in the *Washington Post* newspaper.

# JAZZ

See NIGHTLIFE.

# JEWELRY

**Boone & Sons, Inc.** 1730 K Street, N.W.; 785-4653.
**Charles Schwartz & Son** Mazza Gallerie, 5300 Wisconsin Avenue, N.W.; 363-5432. Also selling sterling and china.
**Dikomey Jewelers** 1725 I Street, N.W. (Farragut Square Metro stop); 872-8088. Jewelry designing, repair, appraisal, remounting; since 1955.
**Discount Wholesalers** 733 13th Street, N.W. (Metro Center Metro stop); 347-6760. Jewelry.
**Galt & Bro., Inc.** 15th and F Streets, N.W. (their new address downtown); 347-1034. Founded 1802, the nation's oldest jewelry store. Also selling sterling and china. Monogramming, sterling, and watch repair.
**Pampillonia** 1213 Connecticut Avenue, N.W. (downtown); 628-6305. Also at Mazza Gallerie, 5300 Wisconsin Avenue, N.W.; 363-6305.
**Tiny Jewel Box** 1143 Connecticut Avenue, N.W.; 393-2747. Antique jewelry.

# KITES

**Kite Site** 3101 M Street, N.W. (Georgetown); 965-4230. Kites and kite-making materials.

**Smithsonian's National Air and Space Museum
Shop** 7th Street and Independence Avenue, S.W.; 357-1387. Kites and twine.

# KITCHENWARES

See HOME AND KITCHEN FURNISHINGS.

# LANDMARKS

See SIGHTS WORTH SEEING.

# LEATHER GOODS AND LUGGAGE

**Camalier & Buckley** 1141 Connecticut Avenue, N.W.; 347-7700. Luggage and luggage repair, handbags, and gifts.
**Coach Leatherware** 1214 Wisconsin Avenue, N.W.; 342-1772. A branch of the famous American-made-leather store in New York. Wallets, briefcases, handbags, belts, and bags for men and women—in classic styles, natural leather, and solid brass.
**Complement** 1652 K Street, N.W.; 833-2295. Also at 1984 M Street, N.W.; 296-4494. Briefcases, attachés, luggage, handbags, gloves, etc. Reasonable prices and lots of sales.
**Georgetown Leather Design** 3265 M Street, N.W.; 333-9333. Also at 1150 Connecticut Avenue, N.W.; 223-1855. Leather and suede jackets, handbags, shoes, boots, and accessories.
**Gucci Washington** Les Champs at the Watergate, 600 New Hampshire Avenue, N.W. (Foggy Bottom); 965-1700.
**Lane's Luggage** 1146 Connecticut Avenue, N.W.; 452-1146. Luggage repair also.
**Mark Cross** Georgetown Park, 3222 M Street, N.W.; 342-2413. Fine luggage, attachés, and small leather goods.

Leather Goods

# LIBRARIES

All are open to the public unless noted. Hours are generally daily 9–5 with the exception of restricted days and hours at society libraries.

**American Institute of Architects** 1735 New York Avenue, N.W. (downtown); 626-7300.

**Columbia Historical Society Library** 1307 New Hampshire Avenue, N.W. at N Street (Dupont Circle); 785-2068. History of Washington, D.C. Open Wednesday, Friday, and Saturday, noon–4 PM.

**Dumbarton Oaks** 1703 32nd Street, N.W. (Georgetown); Pre-Columbian Library, 342-3265; Byzantine Library, 342-3240; Garden Library, 342-3280. Open only to qualified scholars.

**John F. Kennedy Center Library** For the Performing Arts of the Library of Congress, at the Kennedy Center Roof Terrace, North Gallery; 287-6245. Exhibits, video, and cassette tapes and recordings. Tuesday–Friday, 11–8:30; Saturday, 10–6. Closed Sunday, Monday, and holidays.

**Library of Congress** *Thomas Jefferson Building,* 1st Street and Independence Avenue, S.E.; 287-5000. Main Reading Room, Hispanic Reading Room, Rare Book Room, Local History and Genealogy Reading Room, ground floor exhibition hall, Visitors Services Center, and Coolidge Auditorium. Principal reading rooms open Monday–Saturday, 9 AM–5:30 PM; Wednesdays 'til 9 PM. Closed Sundays. Hours, which have been greatly curtailed because of budget cuts, are subject to change. *James Madison Memorial Building,* 101 Independence Avenue, S.E. Copyright Office, Law Library, Mary Pickford Theater, exhibition hall, atrium, cafeteria, and coffee shop. *John Adams Building,* 2nd Street and Independence Avenue, S.E. Art Deco building entrance and murals in the Social Science Reading Room are special attractions. Other reading rooms and hours of service available upon request from Central Services Division. See also SIGHTS—GOVERNMENT IN ACTION.

**Martin Luther King, Jr. Memorial Library** (D.C. Public Library) 901 G Street, N.W. (downtown); 727-1111.

Gallery Place Metro stop. And branches. Open weekends and evenings, Monday–Thursday.

**Mooreland-Spingarn Research Center** Howard University, 6th and College Streets, N.W.; 636-7239. Black culture and heritage; Black African and Caribbean materials. During school year, open evenings and Saturdays.

**National Archives Research Rooms** Pennsylvania Avenue at 8th Street, N.W. (downtown); 523-3204. Genealogical information, etc. Monday–Friday, 9 AM–10 PM; Saturday, 9–5.

**National Geographic Society Library** 16th and M Streets, N.W. (Dupont Circle); 857-7783. Reading rooms open to the public.

**National Library Service for the Blind and Physically Handicapped** 1291 Taylor Street, N.W. (uptown); 287-5100.

**National Society of the Daughters of the American Revolution Library** 1776 D Street, N.W. (downtown); 628-1776. $5/day to nonmembers of DAR and related societies; $2/day between 11:30–1:30. Monday–Friday, 9–4. Family history, genealogy.

**Society of the Cincinnati** Anderson House, 2118 Massachusetts Avenue, N.W. (Dupont Circle); 785-0540. Genealogy.

# LIMOUSINES

See TRANSPORTATION.

# LIQUOR

See BARS AND PUBS; WINES AND LIQUORS.

# LUGGAGE

See LEATHER GOODS AND LUGGAGE.

# MAGAZINES

See NEWSPAPERS AND MAGAZINES.

# MAPS OF THE CITY

Whether you are driving a car, using public transportation, or "hoofing it," the following maps would be very helpful:

**Washington, D.C.** Published for free distribution by the District of Columbia Department of Transportation; available at the Tourist Information Center (see INFORMATION). This map includes tips on driving safely in Washington. Be aware of all parking signs and obey hours posted in tow-away zones. If your car is towed, call 727-5000 to locate your car.

**Flashmaps, Instant Guide to Washington** Available in bookstores, this pocketbook gives subway and bus routes; maps showing theaters, hotels, restaurants, and museums; and emergency numbers and much more.

**Free Visitor Maps** are published by the Washington, D.C. Convention and Visitors Association. Available at Tourist Information Center (see INFORMATION).

**Guide to the Nation's Capital and the Smithsonian Institution** is a fold-out map of the core of Washington including information on places of interest. Available at the Smithsonian Bookstore, National Museum of American History, $1.

**The Map Store** 1636 I Street, N.W.; 628-2608. At the top of Farragut West Metro stop (17th Street exit) and near Farragut North Metro stop. Closed Saturdays except during December. Sells the latest in handy maps to Washington, as well as guides.

**The News Room** 1753 Connecticut Avenue (Dupont Circle Metro stop); 332-1489. Terrific selection of guidebooks and maps to Washington and other cities. Open daily and 'til late in the evening.

**Tourist Washington** Map published March 1983 by the National Geographic Society and available from their sales desk at 17th and M Streets, N.W. Printed on water-resistant paper, $1. (See the January 1983 issue of *National Geographic* for a larger version of the same map.)

# MEDICAL CARE

See HOSPITALS AND HEALTH EMERGENCIES.

# MEN'S CLOTHING

See HABERDASHERIES AND TAILORS.

# MONEY EXCHANGE (FOR FOREIGNERS)

See INFORMATION.

# MOTELS

See HOTELS AND MOTELS.

# MOVIE THEATERS (OUT OF THE ORDINARY)

Review the "Weekend" section of Friday's *Washington Post* for an up-to-date report of movies at the various repertory theaters. The *Washington Post* and the *Washington Times* list movies at area theaters daily.
**American Film Institute Theater** Kennedy Center; 785-4600. Open to nonmembers on a space-available basis.
**Biograph** 2819 M Street, N.W.; 333-2696. Showing classic films, many film festivals.
**Circle Theater** 2105 Pennsylvania Avenue, N.W.; 331-7480. Oldies but goodies in a double feature at a very reasonable price. Ask for their calendar. Very popular and often sold out especially in the evening.
**Hirshhorn Museum and Sculpture Garden** Independence Avenue at Eighth Street, S.W.; 357-2700. Lunchtime films about art and artists; Saturday films for young people at 11 AM; evening films by artist film-

makers at 8 PM. Shown in the Museum's auditorium, lower level. Consult the Museum's calendar of events for schedule. Free.

**Mary Pickford Theater** Library of Congress, James Madison Building, Independence Avenue at 1st Street, S.E., 3rd floor; 287-5677. Classics shown in an intimate, comfortable, 64-seat theater. Telephone reservations should be made a week in advance. Doors open 30 minutes before showtime; standbys admitted 10 minutes before showtime. Varied schedule announced in quarterly newsletter sent to mailing list and in Friday's *Washington Post* "Weekend" section. Free.

**National Gallery of Art** East Building, 4th Street at Constitution Avenue, N.W.; 737-4215. Shown in the auditorium are films on art and feature films related to special exhibitions. Seating unreserved. Free.

**Samuel Langley Theater** National Air and Space Museum, 7th Street and Independence Avenue, N.W. (L'Enfant Plaza Metro stop, Maryland Avenue and 7th Street exit); 357-2700. Besides the series of films shown daily on the IMAX screen, special showings of new and classic films occur on selected evenings. Watch the newspapers and museum's calendar of events for announcements.

**Summer Cinema at The National** 1321 Pennsylvania Avenue, N.W., 20004; 783-3372. Classic movies are shown in the Helen Hayes Gallery Monday evenings, 7 PM, during June and July. For the schedule, send a long self-addressed stamped envelope. Reservations required. Free.

**Washington Project for the Arts** 400 7th Street, N.W.; 347-8304. Special films and videos.

# MUSEUMS

For up-to-date listings of events at each of the museums, check newspapers and/or magazine features.

The Washington Convention and Visitors Association publishes a list of museums in *Washington, D.C.: A Capital City!* and highlights current exhibits and other events in *Calendar of Events*, published quar-

NATURAL HISTORY MUSEUM OF
SMITHSONIAN INSTITUTION

terly and available at the Tourist Information Center.
(See INFORMATION.)

A calendar of events is often available at each museum. (See INFORMATION.)

Note that many museums have excellent restaurants or cafeterias. (See RESTAURANTS.) Museums in

**Museums**

Washington are also well-known for their unique selection of souvenirs, gifts, toys, books, and clothes.

**Most of these museums are open daily 10 AM
to 5:30 PM and are closed Thanksgiving, Christmas, and New Year's Day.** The smaller private museums are open weekdays and closed on federal holidays.

For museums of special interest to children, see
CHILDREN AND CHILDREN'S THINGS. All are free unless
noted and are accessible to the handicapped. (See
HANDICAPPED INDIVIDUALS' RESOURCES.)

Tours are generally given daily but are by appointment in the smaller private museums. **Dupont Kalorama Museums Consortium** includes the Phillips
Collection, Textile Museum, Woodrow Wilson House,
Anderson House, Columbia Historical Society, Barney
Studio House, and Fondo Del Sol Visual Art and Media
Center. An elaborate brochure published by the Consortium includes a very clear map of the *Dupont Kalorama Museum Walk* and includes hotels and galleries in the neighborhood. For a copy of the brochure by
mail, send a stamped self-addressed long envelope to
the Consortium at 1600 21st Street, N.W., Washington, D.C. 20009; 387-2151.

The Consortium is emphasized here because so
often the tourist is drawn to the Mall and entirely
misses these fine galleries, museums, and the Kalorama neighborhood, which introduce the visitor to the
non–federal-government, more personal side of Washington. The Phillips Collection and the Textile Museum are described below; Fondo del Sol is described
under ART GALLERIES; and Anderson House, Columbia
Historical Society, and Woodrow Wilson House are described under SIGHTS—LANDMARKS AND HISTORIC
HOMES.

## Art Museums

**Arthur M. Sackler Gallery** 1050 Independence Avenue, S.W. (Smithsonian Metro stop); 357-1300. The
collections of Near Eastern and Asian art in the Sackler Gallery span very early cultures through the 20th
century and complement the collections at the adjacent Freer Gallery. The Sackler Gallery includes loan
exhibitions and major international shows, accompa-

nied by public programs and scholarly symposia. Advanced research scholarship and educational programs are enhanced by the library located in the Sackler Gallery and shared with the Freer Gallery. This museum is part of the Smithsonian Institution and will open June 1987.

**Barney Studio House** 2306 Massachusetts Avenue, N.W.; 357-2700. Special concerts and exhibits. For details see SIGHTS—LANDMARKS AND HISTORIC HOMES.

**Corcoran Gallery of Art** 17th Street and New York Avenue, N.W. (downtown); 638-3211. Closed Monday. Open Thursday 'til 9 PM. Traditional and contemporary American art. Opened in 1897.

**Dumbarton Oaks** 1703 32nd Street, N.W. (Georgetown); 338-8278. A quiet museum housing Robert Woods Bliss Pre-Columbian collection in a small, circular, glass-walled addition designed by Philip Johnson. This is also the home of the well-known Byzantine Collection. Dumbarton Oaks has several libraries open to qualified scholars (see LIBRARIES), a music room (see MUSIC), and a lovely garden (see PARKS AND NATURE PRESERVES). Closed Monday; other days, 2–5 PM. Suggested admission.

**Freer Gallery of Art** 12th Street and Jefferson Drive, S.W. (on the Mall; next to the Smithsonian Metro stop); 357-2700. A quiet museum exhibiting a large, famous collection of Oriental art and the largest collection of art by James A. McNeill Whistler. This is part of the Smithsonian Institution.

**Hirshhorn Museum and Sculpture Garden** Independence Avenue at 8th Street, S.W. (on the Mall; L'Enfant Plaza Metro stop, Maryland Avenue and 7th Street exit); 357-2700. Nineteenth- and 20th-century American and European art including sculpture. Plaza Cafe serves simple sandwiches and salads in the summertime. This is part of the Smithsonian Institution.

**Library of Congress** 1st Street between Independence Avenue and East Capitol Street, S.E.; 287-5458. Extensive collection of prints (dating from the 15th century) and photographs in the Division of Prints and Photographs; pieces from the collection exhibited in the James Madison Memorial Building Cafeteria. (See LIBRARIES.)

**Museum of Modern Art of Latin America** 201 18th Street, N.W. (downtown); 789-6016. Also the Organization of American States, 17th Street at Constitution Avenue, N.W. The museum has a collection of Latin American contemporary art. There is a room devoted to the forerunners of Latin American art and a room devoted to the native art of Latin America. A lovely Aztec garden joins this museum to the OAS gallery showing temporary exhibits.

**National Gallery of Art** Constitution Avenue at 6th Street, N.W. (Archives Metro stop); general information, 737-4215; information about special exhibitions, 842-6699 or 842-6672. Sunday hours, noon to 9 PM. Late medieval and early Renaissance European art through post-impressionism and American art in the West Building; American and European contemporary art and traveling exhibitions in the East Building. See NGA's Calendar of Events for weekly tours, films, lectures, and concerts. Marvelous cafeteria and cafes. Open until 4:30 PM Monday–Saturday and until 6 PM Sunday. Concert in West Garden Court Sundays at 7 PM.

**National Museum of African Art** 950 Independence Avenue, S.W.; 357-1300. This is the only museum in the United States devoted to the collection, exhibition, and study of African art. Approximately 5 major exhibits each year. The collection itself includes 6,000 works of art, primarily from sub-Saharan Africa. A resident fellowship program makes the collection and research facilities available for advanced scholarly research. The Eliot Elisofon Archives consists of 140,000 slides and black-and-white negatives, and 100,000 feet of unedited film footage on African art. Opens June 1987. This is part of the Smithsonian Institution.

**National Museum of American Art** 8th and G Streets, N.W. (downtown; Gallery Place Metro stop); 357-2700. American art of the 18th, 19th and 20th centuries, including a very large collection of American Indian paintings by George Catlin. NMAA shares the Old Patent Office Building with the National Portrait Gallery to the south; in the center is a lovely courtyard where you can enjoy your lunch or tea bought at Patent Pending, a small cafe adjoining the 2 museums, serving soup, sandwiches, and wine. Walk-in tours weekdays at noon and Sundays at 1:45 PM. This is part of the Smithsonian Institution.

**National Museum of Women in the Arts** 801 13th

Street, N.W. (between New York Avenue and H Street, N.W., Metro Center Metro stop, 13th Street exit); 337-2615. (Through early 1987 the address is 4590 MacArthur Boulevard, N.W.; 337-2615.) Located in a recently renovated Renaissance Revival building, the museum focuses on the contributions of women to the history of art through acquisitions, research, interpretation, and exhibitions. Monday–Friday, 10–5 PM.

**National Portrait Gallery** F Street at 8th Street, N.W. (downtown; Gallery Place Metro stop); 357-2700. Portraits and busts of famous Americans from presidents to musicians; interesting temporary exhibits. Patent Pending cafe adjoins the NPG to the National Museum of American Art. This is part of the Smithsonian Institution.

**Phillips Collection** 1600 21st Street, N.W. (Dupont Circle); 387-2151. Visitor information recording: 387-0961. American and European modern art is exhibited in this quiet gallery, formerly the home of Marjorie and Duncan Phillips. Free concerts Sunday at 5 in the music room from September through late May or early June. Elevator and ramps provide the handicapped with access to the museum. Educational programs. Tearoom serves light snacks. Free tours Wednesday and Saturday at 2 PM. Suggested admission. Closed Monday. Member, Dupont Kalorama Museums Consortium.

**Renwick Gallery** Of the National Museum of American Art, Pennsylvania Avenue at 17th Street, N.W. (downtown); 357-2700. Temporary exhibitions of work by American craftsmen and designers. Frequent films and lectures. Farragut West Metro stop. This is part of the Smithsonian Institution.

**Textile Museum** 2320 S Street, N.W. (Dupont Circle Metro stop); 667-0441. Closed Monday. Antique rugs and textiles from all over the world exhibited in this pleasant, quiet museum a few blocks west of the Phillips Collection. Nice gift shop. Suggested admission. Member, Dupont Kalorama Museums Consortium.

# Historical and Scientific Museums

**Armed Forces Medical Museum** 6825 16th Street, N.W., Armed Forces Institute of Pathology, Building

#54 (Walter Reed Army Hospital); 576-2418. Exhibits on the evolution and effects of disease. Established 1862.

**B'Nai B'Rith Klutznick Museum** 1640 Rhode Island Avenue, N.W. (Dupont Circle); 857-6583. Permanent collection of Jewish ceremonial art; special exhibits and the Judaica Museum Shop. Sunday through Friday, 10–5. Closed Saturday, Jewish holidays, and national holidays. Open December 25.

**Daughters of the American Revolution Museum** 1776 D Street, N.W. (downtown); 628-1776. Thirty period rooms and collection of American decorative art from 1700 to 1850. Weekdays, 9–4; Sunday, 1–5; closed Saturday. Free. See also LIBRARIES; CHILDREN AND CHILDREN'S THINGS—MUSEUMS.

**Lincoln Museum at Ford's Theatre** 511 10th Street, N.W. (downtown); 426-6924. President Abraham Lincoln was assassinated in Ford's Theatre April 14, 1865. The museum contains items related to the Lincolns and to assassin John Wilkes Booth. The theatre is much the same as it was in 1865 and is on view to the public except during performances and rehearsals. (See THEATERS.)

**Marine Corps Museum** Building #58, Washington Navy Yard, 9th and M Streets Gate, S.E.; 433-3534. Exhibits showing the history of the U.S. Marine Corps from 1775 to the present. Closed Christmas and New Year's days.

**NASA Goddard Space Flight Center** Greenbelt, Md. 20771; 344-8101 or 344-8981. Full-scale collection of rockets and satellites and film clips of recent space flights. Model rocket launch 1st and 3rd Sundays at 1:30. Gallery hours are Wednesday–Sunday, 10–4; tour Thursdays at 2 PM. Directions: Take the Baltimore-Washington Parkway to Exit 22A and proceed to the Goddard Space Flight Center, following signs.

**National Archives** 8th Street and Constitution Avenue, N.W. (downtown); 523-3000. Declaration of Independence, Constitution, and Bill of Rights. See information under LIBRARIES for reference services.

**National Building Museum** In the Pension Building, F Street between 4th and 5th Streets, N.W. (Judiciary Square Metro stop, F Street exit); 272-2448. Exhibits highlight building in America, past, present, and future. The Old Pension Building, designed by General

Montgomery Meigs in 1881, was recently mandated by Congress to commemorate and encourage the American building arts. Monday–Friday, 10–4. Saturday, Sunday, and holidays, noon–4. Lunchtime concerts and Sunday films on buildings and other architectural structures. Tours offered.

**National Geographic Society** Explorers Hall, 17th and M Streets, N.W.; 857-7588. Exhibits of land, sea, and space. Excellent maps and books sold here at very reasonable prices. See also LIBRARIES.

**Naval Memorial Museum** Washington Navy Yard, 9th and M Streets, S.E.; 433-2651. Heritage and scientific and diplomatic achievements of the U.S. Navy.

**Smithsonian Institution** Call 357-2700 for information on all museums. Open daily, 10–5:30. Closed Christmas Day. See also MUSEUMS—ART MUSEUMS, where you will find the Smithsonian art museums listed under their individual names. Listed below are the historic and scientific museums of the Smithsonian Institution:

**ANACOSTIA NEIGHBORHOOD MUSEUM** 2405 Martin Luther King Avenue at Talbert Avenue, S.E. Afro-American history and culture. Monday–Friday, 10–6 and weekends, 1–6.

**ARTS AND INDUSTRIES BUILDING** 9th Street and Jefferson Drive, S.W. Four exhibit halls are filled with an extensive collection of Victorian Americana simulating the Philadelphia Exposition of 1876. Included are working steam engines, 1876 Baldwin locomotive, cut glass, and home furnishings. Unusual gift shop. Tours by appointment and require 2 days' notice.

**EDUCATION CENTER** Entrance is through the kiosk located between the Castle building and the Freer Gallery. Here are classrooms and a public lecture hall for use by Smithsonian groups, including the National and Resident Associate programs. Opens June 1987.

**INTERNATIONAL CENTER** Entrance is through the kiosk located between the Castle building and the Freer Gallery. The Center sponsors research, scholarly and public symposia, and exhibitions focusing on all cultures of the world, especially the non-Western world. Programs will explore ancient and evolving cultures and serve as headquarters for Latin American scholarship, exhibitions, and programs. Opens June 1987.

**NATIONAL AIR AND SPACE MUSEUM** 7th Street and Independence Avenue, S.W. The most visited museum in the world exhibits the evolution of aviation and space technology. Special films on flight in the Samuel E. Langley Theater (IMAX screen) and presentations in the Albert Einstein Spacearium are shown daily and should not be missed.

**NATIONAL MUSEUM OF AMERICAN HISTORY** 14th Street and Constitution Avenue, N.W. Here are the First Ladies' gowns, the "Star Spangled Banner," Bell's telephone, Ford's Model T, Whitney's model of the original cotton gin and the Foulcault Pendulum.

**NATIONAL MUSEUM OF NATURAL HISTORY** 10th Street and Constitution Avenue, N.W. Exhibits concentrate on people and their natural surroundings, and range from the mounted African bush elephant, coral reef, and dinosaurs to the Hope Diamond. Here too are the Insect Zoo, Discovery Room, and Naturalist Center set up especially for children. (For these special rooms free tickets are distributed at the Information Desk in the Rotunda on weekends and holidays on a first-come, first-served basis. On other days no tickets are required. Call 357-2700 for hours. Group reservations: 357-2747).

**PAUL E. GARBER NATIONAL AIR AND SPACE RESTORATION FACILITY** 3904 Old Silver Hill Road, Suitland, Maryland 20023; 357-2700. This preservation, restoration, and storage facility houses the National Air and Space Museum's reserve collection of historically significant air and space craft. Free tour includes behind-the-scenes look at the restoration workshops where skilled craftsmen are preserving aircraft and other objects. Tours are given Monday–Friday at 10 AM; Saturday–Sunday at 10 AM and 1 PM. Reservation must be made 2 weeks in advance by calling 357-1400 Tuesday–Thursday, 10 AM–3 PM. Directions to the restoration facility will be mailed to you.

**U.S. Naval Observatory** Massachusetts Avenue at 34th Street, N.W., 20390. Call 653-1543 for recorded message giving current information on popular nighttime tours. You may request a descriptive brochure by mail.

**Washington Doll's House and Toy Museum** 5236 44th Street, N.W. (one block west of Wisconsin Avenue between Jenifer and Harrison Streets); 244-0024. A museum of nostalgia, exhibiting a carefully researched collection of dolls' houses, dolls, and antique toys. Dollhouse furniture and accessories for sale. Inquire about catered parties in the museum's party room. Tuesday–Saturday, 10–5; Sunday, noon–5. Closed Monday, Thanksgiving, Christmas, and New Year's Day. Admission charged.

# MUSIC

## Events

Washington has an abundance of outdoor and indoor musical events from classical to bluegrass, many of which are free. The following publications, available at your newsstand, have excellent calendars: the *Washington Post* "Weekend" section published Friday and the "Show" section published Sunday; the *Washingtonian* magazine; and the *Washington Blade*. (See NEWSPAPERS AND MAGAZINES.)

**District Curators** has information on current avant-garde music, dance, theater, and performance arts around town. Call 783-0360.

Exceptional calendars available well in advance of your visit include the *Calendar of Events* (published by Washington Convention and Visitors Association) (see INFORMATION). Concerts, many of which are free, are also listed in the calendars of events published by the National Park Service, the Library of Congress, the National Gallery of Art, the Phillips Collection, the National Museum of American Art, the Folger Shakespeare Library, the Corcoran Gallery, the Dumbarton Oaks Museum, and the Smithsonian Performing Arts (357-1500). Free organ concerts at the Washington National Cathedral are publicized in the "Religion" section of Saturday's *Washington Post*.

During summer months there are free band concerts almost every night of the week at the Jefferson Memorial and West Terrace of the U.S. Capitol. (See *Calendar of Events* published by the Washington Convention and Visitors Association or call the numbers listed below.) The National Cathedral celebrates a free Summer Music Festival on Tuesdays at 8 PM in July and August with visiting musicians such as string quartets and baroque ensembles.

For information on free U.S. Navy Band concerts, call 433-2394; U.S. Army Band concerts, call 692-7219; U.S. Air Force Band concerts, call 767-5658/4310; U.S. Marine Band concerts, call 433-4492. See INFORMATION—CALENDARS OF EVENTS for further information.

The following musical groups offer programs throughout the year and have a calendar of events:

**Choral Arts Society of Washington** 4321 Wisconsin Avenue, N.W., Washington, D.C. 20016; 244-3669.

**The National Symphony Orchestra** John F. Kennedy Center for the Performing Arts, Washington, D.C. 20566; 785-8100.

**Smithson String Quartet** and the **Smithsonian Chamber Players** perform in the Hall of Musical Instruments and offer a wide-ranging program of music on original instruments. Call the Smithsonian Resident Associates for information on how to obtain tickets: 357-3030.

**Washington Opera** John F. Kennedy Center for the Performing Arts, Washington, D.C. 20566; 223-4757.

See also NIGHTLIFE for nightclubs known for their music.

Following are major spaces in Washington and its environs where notable musicians perform (see also THEATERS).

**The Barns of the Wolf Trap Foundation** 1635 Trap Road, Vienna, Va. 22180; 938-2404. Fall, winter and spring program. Opera for 3 weeks in the summer. *All* styles of music are represented in the programs. For further information and directions see this listing under THEATERS.

**Capital Centre** 1 Harry S. Truman Drive, Landover, Md.; 350-3900. From the Capital Beltway, Route 495, take Exit 15A or 17A and follow the signs. From downtown Washington allow 1 hour in rush-hour traffic. At other times, allow 30 minutes. Not accessible by public transportation. Tickets available at Hecht's and Ticketron.

**Carter Baron Amphitheater** 16th Street and Colorado Avenue, N.W. (uptown); Dial-a-Park, 426-6975. Free concerts for all ages every weekend from late June to

Labor Day sponsored by the National Park Service. Events are listed in the "Weekend" section of Friday's *Washington Post.* Go north on 16th Street to Colorado Avenue or take Rock Creek Park to Blagden Avenue to Colorado Avenue to the main gate.

**DAR Constitution Hall** 18th and D Streets, N.W. (downtown); 638-2661.

**Filene Center II** Wolf Trap Park for the Performing Arts, 1551 Trap Road, Vienna, Va. 22180; 703/255-1860. For performances in the evening at the Filene Center, the Wolf Trap Exit from the Dulles Airport Access Road is open 2 hours before the performance. Other times go west on Leesburg Pike (Route 7) in Virginia to the Wolf Trap Park sign and turn left. Events here are published in Sunday's *Washington Post* and you may request a calendar of events. Not accessible by public transportation.

**John F. Kennedy Center for the Performing Arts** 2700 F Street, N.W. (Foggy Bottom Metro stop); general information, 254-3600. Ticket information for the Concert Hall: 254-3776; for the Opera House: 254-3770; for the Eisenhower Theater: 254-3670; and for the Terrace Theater: 254-9895. Instant-Charge: 857-0900.

**Lisner Auditorium on the George Washington University Campus** 21st Street, N.W. at H Street (downtown. Foggy Bottom Metro stop); 676-6800.

**Smithsonian Performing Arts Events** are held at the following: *Baird Auditorium:* Museum of Natural History, 10th Street and Constitution Avenue, N.W.; *Discovery Theater:* Arts & Industries Building, 900 Jefferson Drive, S.W.; *Hall of Musical Instruments:* Museum of American History, 14th Street and Constitution Avenue, N.W.; *Hirshhorn Auditorium:* Hirshhorn Museum & Sculpture Garden, 7th Street & Independence Avenue, S.W.: *Renwick Grand Salon:* Renwick Gallery, 17th Street and Pennsylvania Avenue, N.W. Smithsonian Box Office, 357-1500; tickets also available at TicketPlace and the Smithsonian Museum Shops.

**Star Plex** D.C. Armory, 2001 East Capitol Street, S.E. (Stadium-Armory Metro stop); event and ticket information, 547-9077. Events are well advertised.

**Music**

## Instruments and Lessons

See the D.C. Yellow Pages for stores in the suburbs selling sheet music.

**Guitar Shop** 1216 Connecticut Avenue, N.W. (between M and N Streets); 331-7333. Guitars, sheet music, and lessons.

**Jordan-Kitt's Music, Inc.** 1330 G Street, N.W. (downtown); 393-6565. Piano and organ sales and lessons.

**Music Box Center** 918 F Street, N.W. (in the National Union Building); 783-9399. Area's largest selection, including antiques. Repairs, replacements, and movements. Here you will also find lessons in organ, piano, and voice taught by Rudy Lewis and staff.

**The Piano Shop** 1117 14th Street, N.W.; 737-7800. An unusual business of selling new, used, and antique pianos (for the past 25 years) and now selling antique furniture as well.

## The Best Jukeboxes in Town

The selection is not as varied as it was a few years ago, but you can still see a Wurlitzer Bubbler, *c.* 1940, on display at the Brickskeller. The following establishments with jukeboxes are listed under various headings: BARS AND PUBS—Brickskeller, Millie & Al's, Tune Inn, and Stetson's Tex-Mex Saloon; GAY SCENE—Mr. Henry's, on Capitol Hill; NIGHTLIFE—One Step Down; RESTAURANTS—Childe Harrold, Timberlake's.

# NATURE PRESERVES

See PARKS AND NATURE PRESERVES.

# NEIGHBORHOODS

To appreciate Washington in another way, move beyond the Mall and sample the diverse neighborhoods: the gentility of **Kalorama** (in the vicinity of the Textile Museum) and of **Embassy Row** on Massachusetts Avenue, where you will find the Vice-Presidential mansion at Observatory Circle, as well as the British Embassy; the ethnic neighborhood of **Adams Morgan**

(18th Street and Columbia Road, N.W.), which is popular with Asians, Hispanics, blacks, and whites; and **Georgetown** (around Wisconsin Avenue and M Street, N.W.), originally laid out in 1751 and resplendent in Federal and Victorian architecture, now well-known for its colorful commercial areas. **Capitol Hill** has over the last 20 years experienced a new lease on life with the renovation of many homes and an influx of nice shops, markets, galleries, restaurants, and hotels.

Washington's **Chinatown** (in the vicinity of 6th and H Streets, N.W.), with its Chinese street signs and pagoda-style telephone booths, looks forward to a revitalization phase motivated by the proximity of the Convention Center. **Le Droit Park** at Florida and Rhode Island Avenues, N.W. near Howard University, consists of many fine homes built by James McGill in the 1870s in the Italian villa, Second Empire shingle, and Gothic cottage romantic styles of this period. Highlighting the **Southwest Waterfront** is the wharf where families of fishermen stand in their floating markets hawking their fresh array of the day's catch. A favorite is the live Chesapeake crabs by the dozen or bushel to take home and steam yourself! Be sure to remember the mallets and bay seasoning.

"Hometown Washington, D.C." in the January 1983 issue of *National Geographic* gives a detailed story of Washington as the residents know it. "The Celebrated City" (from the *Washington Post Magazine, The Washington Post*, February 2, 1986) is a look at how Washington has developed in the last 25 years.

# NEWSPAPERS AND MAGAZINES

**Museum Washington** 2550 M Street, N.W., Suite 405, 20037; 429-6575. A bimonthly magazine covering in detail current and upcoming shows at *all* the museums and galleries in Washington. Each issue includes a feature story on one of the major shows in the city; recommended shows; a guidebook-style section with maps; a description of each museum; and a section especially for children.

**Regardie's** 1010 Wisconsin Avenue, N.W., Suite 600, Washington, D.C. 20007; 342-0410. A monthly magazine about the business of Washington.

**Washington Blade Newspaper** 930 F Street, N.W., Washington, D.C. 20004; 347-2038. Weekly gay community news and events.

**Washington Consumers Checkbook** and **Bargains** 806 15th Street, N.W., Suite 925, Washington, D.C. 20005; 347-9612. Quarterly publications; *Checkbook* rates the prices and quality of goods and services in the Washington area; *Bargains* compares the best prices for specific products sold in the area.

**Washingtonian Magazine** 1828 L Street, N.W., Washington, D.C. 20036; 296-3600. Monthly. Well recommended; calendars of events for galleries, museums, theater, children, sports, etc.

**Washington Monthly** 2712 Ontario Road, N.W., Washington, D.C., 20009; 462-0128. The purpose of this thought-provoking magazine is to "describe how the political system really works, to determine why it succeeds, and why it fails; and to suggest ways in which it might be improved."

**Washington Post** 1150 15th Street, N.W.; Washington, D.C. 20071; 334-6000. Daily. Friday's issue contains "Weekend," listing events in the city and suburbs.

**Washington Review** Lansburgh Cultural Center, 420 7th Street, N.W.; 638-0515. (P.O. Box 50132, Washington, D.C. 20004). Bimonthly tabloid journal of the arts and literature in Washington.

**Washington Times** 3600 New York Avenue, N.E., Washington, D.C. 20002; 636-3000. Daily.

**Washington Woman** 1911 N. Ft. Meyer Drive, Suite 1010, Arlington, Va. 22209; 522-3477. Monthly magazine emphasizing financial planning, Washington women, arts and business calendars, and travel information.

## Newsstands

These newsstands have been selected because they carry a broad range of local, national, and international newspapers and periodicals.

**B and B News Stand** 2621 Connecticut Avenue, N.W. (Woodley Park/Zoo Metro stop); 234-0494. Foreign-language periodicals and newspapers from 80 cities. Also prepackaged food and fresh flowers. Open late.

**Investment Building News Stand** 1511 K Street, N.W. (downtown); 347-1432. International, New York, and local newspapers and magazines.

**News Room** 1753 Connecticut Avenue, N.W. (Dupont Circle Metro stop); 332-1489. Papers and magazines of all descriptions from all over the world. Also books, terrific greeting cards, and an excellent assortment of guidebooks and maps to Washington and other cities. Postcards too! Open late daily. Browsers are welcome as long as they are neat.

**Periodicals** At 3 locations: McPherson Square Metro stop, 898-1998; Farragut West Metro stop, 223-2526; and in Georgetown at 3109 M Street, N.W., 333-6115. Local, national, and international newspapers, magazines, journals, postcards, maps, and foreign language tapes. Selection varies at each location.

**Waldenbooks** 17th Street and Pennsylvania Avenue, N.W.; 393-1490. This branch has an excellent selection of foreign newspapers and magazines.

# NIGHTLIFE

Nighttime entertainment includes comedy shows, belly dancing, moonlight cruises, dancing (even a place to do the Texas two-step), jazz, punk, and folk.

Information on current shows may be found in the *Washington Post*'s "Weekend" section published Fridays and in the "Show" section published Sundays. Other good sources are the *Washington Times* newspaper and the *Washingtonian*, published monthly. See also BARS AND PUBS; MUSIC; THEATER.

Most places have special prices for drinks during the cocktail hour, also known as the "hungry hour," with free munchies; especially weekdays 4–6:30 or so. Regular hours are generally 5 PM to 1, 2, or 3 AM. Places with menus are at least open by lunchtime.

Remember to verify the information given here and to inquire about cover charges.

## Capitol Hill

**Dubliner** 4 F Street, N.W.; 737-3773. Irish folk music. Very popular.

## Southwest

**East Side** 1824 Half Street, S.W.; 488-1205. Brand new "real hot party-dance-entertainment club" says the owner. Two rooms feature 18-foot ceilings with live music in one and dance/rock/video in the other.

**Old Vat Room at Arena Stage** 6th and M Streets, S.W.; 488-3300. Arena's cabaret; light food and cash bar. Shows Thursday through Sunday. Make reservations. Stephen Wade's "Banjo Dancing" has been the popular attraction for years.

**Washington Boat Lines, Inc.** 602 Water Street, S.W., Pier 4; 554-8000. From June through October; there are dance cruises on the Potomac. Live music. *The First Lady*, a triple-deck paddle wheeler, is available for charter or tour cruises.

## Downtown

**The Bank** 915 F Street, N.W.; 393-3632. The newest, ritziest nightclub in town features distinctive music on each of 3 levels: top 40 and Eurodisco; video scenes; and jazz. This is the place to wear your coolest duds. The review in the *Washington Post* says you may want to stop by your *other* bank first! Lunch, Monday–Friday. Nightclub, Wednesday–Sunday.

**Chez Artiste** 1201 Pennsylvania Avenue, N.W. (Metro Center or Federal Triangle Metro stop); 737-7772. French restaurant-supper club featuring musical political satire, cabaret revue, and piano. Shows vary from week to week. Popular entertainment includes the Capitol Steps and Cabaret Americain. Be sure to call ahead to inquire about show and cover charges (if any) and to make reservations. Dinner entrees, $14–18.

**d.c. space** 443 7th Street, N.W. (Gallery Place Metro stop); 347-4960. A gathering space for artists and people who work in galleries. Jazz, punk, theater, art shows, and movie festivals.

**J.J. Mellon's** 1201 Pennsylvania Avenue, N.W.; 737-5700. Several entertainment areas, featuring repertory comedy, live jazz so far. American cuisine including grilled seafood. Lunch, Monday–Friday; dinner, Monday–Saturday; closed Sunday. ($9–18)

**9:30 Club** 930 F Street, N.W. (Gallery Place and Metro Center Metro stops); 638-2008. An "in" place featuring local and out-of-town bands popular with the early 20's crowd.

**One Step Down** 2517 Pennsylvania Avenue, N.W. (Foggy Bottom Metro stop); 331-8863. Small, relaxed jazz club; live music begins around 10 PM; jazz on the jukebox at other times. Sidewalk cafe open seasonally.

# Georgetown and Glen Echo

**Bayou** 3131 K Street, N.W. (under the Freeway); 333-2897. Live entertainment from punk to folk. Tickets at Ticketron and at the Bayou. Hors d'oeuvres and pizza served.

**Blues Alley** No. 1 Blues Alley (at the rear of 1703 Wisconsin Avenue, N.W.); 337-4141. Washington's best spot for jazz; 2 or 3 shows every night; internationally known musicians; Creole cuisine; reservations suggested.

**Fish Market** 1054 31st Street, N.W. in Canal Square; 342-1188. Ragtime and nostalgia music on the piano. Four different entertainment areas here.

**Garvin's Comedy Club** In the Fish Market, 1054 31st Street, N.W. in Canal Square; 726-1334. Comedy every Friday and Saturday night, 8:30 and 10:30. Food and drinks.

**Glen Echo Spanish Ballroom** At Glen Echo Park, 7000 block of MacArthur Boulevard and Goldsboro Road in Maryland; 492-6282. On Fridays, square dancing; Saturdays, folk dancing; and Sundays, big-band ballroom dancing beginning at 8:30. Admission $3. Beginners welcome; inquire about free lessons given before 8:30.

**Oxford Club Restaurant** 3340 M Street, N.W.; 342-3855. A 3-level restaurant including a basement lounge, second-floor dining area, and street-level room with a comfortable atmosphere where people can listen to live jazz.

**Poseurs** 3401 M Street, N.W.; 965-5600. New music video dance club. Monday, guest VJ night; Sunday night, drinks $1; Wednesday, gentlemen's night; Thursday, ladies' night.

## Upper Wisconsin Avenue (Tenley Circle/Friendship Heights)

**Babes** 4226 Wisconsin Avenue, N.W.; 686-1000. Reasonable prices and varied menu, including the best ribs in town and "choose-your-own" lobster. Outside cafe and carryout. Live entertainment, with infrequent cover and minimum charges. Open for lunch Monday–Saturday and for dinner on Sunday.

## Lower Connecticut Avenue/Dupont Circle

This area is wall-to-wall restaurants, discos, and bars. Metro stations serving this area are Dupont Circle and Farragut North. Here are a few places:

**Astor** 1813 M Street, N.W.; 331-7994. This Greek restaurant features belly dancing at 8:30 and 11 PM nightly.

**Bronco Billie's Good Time Saloon** 1821½ L Street, N.W.; 887-5141. Real cowboy with live music Tuesday–Sunday; "oldies," rhythm & blues, and rock & roll, Monday. Every Wednesday, dance lessons from 4:30–9 PM and dance contests with big prizes. Happy hour 4:30–8:30 weekdays with different buffets each day such as seafood, Italian, Mexican, etc.

**Cagney's** One Dupont Circle, N.W.; 659-8820. "New-wave world" with 6-foot video screen, DJ, 18-foot mirror on dance floor, and "love booths." Popular among college kids (domestic and international). Lunch and dinner. Monday night is "Old Wave Night," Cinderella hour starting at midnight. Tuesday is gentlemen's night; Wednesday is ladies' night ($1 drinks); Thursday is "Import Night" (imported beer); Friday and Saturday have a reduced cover before 10 PM.

**Comedy Cafe** 1520 K Street, N.W. (across from the Capitol Hilton); 638-5112. Comedy and jazz. Dinner served. Reservations suggested.

**Deja Vu** 2119 M Street, N.W.; 452-1966. This huge

place considers itself the home of the jitterbug; it sports 3 floorsful of bars and dance floors. Opens at 8:30 PM.

**Food for Thought** 1738 Connecticut Avenue, N.W.; 797-1095. Vegetarian and nonvegetarian. Music is eclectic, i.e., blues acts, "pop," emphasis on acoustic music, folk, and classical guitar.

**Mel Krupin's Lounge** 1120 Connecticut Avenue, N.W.; 331-7000. Distinct from Mel's restaurant, the lounge is open for lunch and 'til the early morning hours Monday–Saturday, with piano on Friday and Saturday evenings. "After-Theater Snacks" menu. No cover and no minimum. Closed Sunday.

**Mirage** 1330 19th Street, N.W.; 463-8888. New York-style dance club. Themes change every 12 weeks. Hot new club.

**Rumors** 1900 M Street, N.W.; 466-7378. Popular with singles. Live music on Mondays at M Street and on Wednesday and Saturday at H Street.

## Upper Connecticut Avenue (Woodley Park/Zoo Metro Stop)

**Marquee Lounge at the Shoreham Hotel** 2500 Calvert Street, N.W.; 234-0700. Entertainment varies. Watch for listing in "Guide to the Lively Arts" and elsewhere in the *Washington Post* and the *Washingtonian* magazine.

## Adams Morgan

**Hazel's Lounge & Restaurant** 1834 Columbia Road, N.W.; 462-0415. Serving American Southern cuisine with entrees ranging from $6–14. Live jazz Friday & Saturday.

**Kilimanjaro's Heritage Hall** 1724 California Street, N.W.; 328-3838. Different live sounds here: reggae, African, soul, and calypso. Dancing encouraged.

**Mr. Henry's Adams Morgan** 1836 Columbia Road, N.W.; 797-8882. Live entertainment nightly: Sunday–Tuesday and Thursday, all styles of music on the piano. Wednesday, amateur night—anything but striptease! Friday and Saturday, "Julia & Co." singing all styles. Serving American cuisine for lunch and dinner. Champagne brunch on Sunday, 11–3.

## Georgia Avenue

**Woodie's Hill Top Pub** 2718 Georgia Avenue, N.W.; 232-2681. Good food, lower than usual prices, and great jazz musicians. If jazz is your interest, you must not miss Woodie's.

# PARKS AND NATURE PRESERVES

Good reference material is in *Natural Washington* and *Spring in Washington*, listed under BOOKS—GUIDE-BOOKS TO WASHINGTON.

**Bishops Garden** Washington National Cathedral. Here you can sit peacefully among the fragrant English boxwood and view the city from one of the highest points.

**Botanic Gardens of the U.S.** 1st and Canal Streets, S.W. at Maryland Avenue; 225-8333. This oversized greenhouse sits just below the Capitol and offers a nice change of pace while sightseeing in the area. Especially during holiday seasons there are beautiful floral plant exhibits. Outdoor garden features perennials, annuals, flowering bulbs, and flowering shrubs, all labeled.

**C&O Canal Park** Thomas Jefferson Street, N.W. in Georgetown just west of M Street. The canal extends 184.5 miles into Cumberland, Maryland. During the summer, the National Capital Park Service offers rides on old-fashioned mule-drawn canal boats. A costumed crew recreates—through conversation, story, and song—life along the canal in 1876. Rides lasting 1½ hours begin mid-morning until late afternoon on "The Georgetown," Wednesdays through Sundays, mid-April through mid-October. Tickets sold at a reasonable fee may be purchased 2 hours in advance of departure from the Foundry Mall Visitor Center, 1055 Thomas Jefferson Place, N.W.; 426-4376. Running parallel to the Potomac River, the canal has an adjacent pathway perfect for walking, biking, and jogging. During winter months, ice skating on the canal is permitted when conditions are safe.

**Dumbarton Oaks Gardens** 31st and R Streets, N.W. (Georgetown); 338-8278. Ten acres of formal terraced gardens designed by Beatrice Farrand. Open daily from 2–5. From April through October, admission is $2/adult, $1/senior citizens and children; seniors free on Wednesdays. No charge from November through March. Closed holidays.

**East Potomac Park** Bounded by the Potomac River to the south and Washington Channel to the east. It is also known as Hains Point, which is actually the southernmost tip of the park. There are a public golf course, swimming pool, picnic grounds, and play equipment for children. The double-flowering cherry trees bloom about a week later than those around the Tidal Basin.

**Enid A. Haupt Garden** A spectacular 3-part garden on 4.2 acres is located between the Smithsonian Castle and Independence Avenue. A Victorian embroidery *parterre* (an ornamental garden with flowers) is one part of the Haupt Garden in the vicinity of the Arts and Industries Building (which displays the 1876 Philadelphia Exposition exhibition). In the vicinity of the Museum of African Art, Arthur M. Sackler Gallery, Freer Gallery, and Smithsonian Residents Kiosk are the Oriental winter and Islamic summer gardens. The plants are identified. Garden furniture and fountains encourage the visitor to take time to enjoy this unique pleasure in the heart of Washington. Opens June 1987.

**Glen Echo Park** MacArthur Boulevard and Goldsboro road, Glen Echo, Md.; 492-6282. Glen Echo began in 1891 as a National Chautauqua Assembly "To promote liberal and practical education. . . ." By 1900 it had become an amusement park with roller coasters and swimming pool. By 1971 it had been organized by the National Park Service to again serve the public by offering in 4 sessions throughout the year a variety of classes in art, theater, dance, photography, and writing to children and adults. On Sundays in the summer there are concerts, demonstrations, workshops, and festivals. For information on the carousel, see CHILDREN AND CHILDREN'S THINGS; for information on dancing in the Spanish Ballroom, see NIGHTLIFE.

**Glover Archbold Park** Extends from Canal Road and 44th Street up toward American University and the

Naval Communications Center on Nebraska Avenue. Hiking and picnicking.

**Hillwood Gardens** 4155 Linnean Avenue, N.W. (uptown); 686-5807. French *parterre* and Japanese garden; greenhouse has many species of orchids. Children under 12, including infants, are not admitted. Open 11–4. Also see SIGHTS WORTH SEEING—OTHER SIGHTS.

**Meridian Hill Park (Malcolm X Park)** 16th Street at Florida Avenue, N.W. Designed in 1920 by Horace Peaslee; this park has a lovely Italian garden where water cascades into lily ponds.

**Montrose Park** Extends from R and 30th Streets up toward the National Zoo. Picnicking and play equipment for children.

**National Arboretum** 24th and R Streets, N.E.; mailing address: 3501 New York Avenue, N.W., Washington, D.C. 20002; 475-4815. Over 400 acres filled with azaleas in the spring; fine collection of Oriental plants, dogwood, and fern, etc. Monday–Friday, 8–5; weekends, 10–5. National Bonsai Collection, weekdays, 10–2:30. Administration and Information Building, weekdays, 8–4:30, and weekends for scheduled events only.

**Normanstone Park** Sits on the northeast side of the Naval Observatory.

**Rock Creek Park** 1,754 acres extending from approximately the Kennedy Center to well beyond the Zoo. Exercise course, bike paths, tennis courts, picnicking, nature trails, stables, and bridle paths. Beach Drive runs through the park. The *Nature Center* at 5200 Glover Road (426-6829) offers educational programs for all ages and features a planetarium with weekend shows. The Nature Center is open Tuesday through Sunday, 9 AM–5 PM. *Peirce Mill* at 2375 Tilden Street and Beach Drive is an 1820s working mill open Wednesday–Sunday, 8–4:30. See CHILDREN AND CHILDREN'S THINGS—PLAYGROUNDS AND PARKS for further information.

**Theodore Roosevelt Island** An 88-acre wilderness preserve on the Potomac River across from the Kennedy Center and Georgetown Waterfront. Go west on Roosevelt Bridge exiting onto the George Washington Memorial Parkway to the north; parking lot is immediately on your right. Foot trails. For tour information, 426-6922.

**Tidal Basin** At the Jefferson Memorial is surrounded by the cherry trees given in friendship by Japan in 1912. They flower in late March or early April. See ANNUAL EVENTS.

**West Potomac Park** Includes the Lincoln Memorial, Reflecting Pool, Constitutional Gardens, Ellipse, Washington Monument, Sylvan Theater, Tidal Basin, and Jefferson Memorial. There are food facilities, information center, ballfields, fishing, and—during the summer—swan boats, rowboats, canoes, and paddleboats for rent at the north bank of the Tidal Basin.

# PASTRY SHOPS

See BAKERIES AND PASTRY SHOPS.

# PERFUME AND TOILETRIES

**Galerie des Parfums, Inc.** 3251 Prospect Street, N.W. (Georgetown); 965-5090. Large variety French and domestic fragrances for ladies and gentlemen.

# PHARMACIES

See DRUGSTORES.

# PHOTOGRAPHY

## Shows, Exhibits, and Galleries

**Kathleen Ewing Gallery** 1609 Connecticut Avenue, N.W., Suite 200; 328-0955. Nineteenth- and early 20th-century and contemporary fine art photography. Member, WADA. (See ART GALLERIES.)

**Woodfin Camp Agency** 925½ F Street, N.W. (downtown); 638-5705. This is the Washington office

TIDAL BASIN WITH
CHERRY BLOSSOMS IN BLOOM

of the New York-based agency representing professional freelance photographers. Many of the photographers in Washington are published in the *National Geographic*.

## Supplies and Equipment

Here are 2 *very good* businesses among the many in this city.

**Baker's Photo Supply, Inc.** 4433 Wisconsin Avenue, N.W. (uptown); 362-9100. Since 1947.

**Penn Camera Exchange, Inc.** 915 E Street, N.W. (downtown); 347-5777.

# PLAYGROUNDS

See CHILDREN AND CHILDREN'S THINGS.

# POETRY

Poets and poetry readings abound in Washington. For events of the week, call 783-POET (783-7638).

**Art Barn** 2401 Tilden Street, N.W.; 426-6719. Evening poetry programs on a Thursday evening once a month.

**The Folger Shakespeare Library** sponsors an evening poetry series, seminars with poets, and the Midday Muse (lunchtime poetry, music, and programs for children on random Thursdays at 12:15 to 1 PM). Call the Poetry Coordinator for a calendar of poetic events, 544-7077.

**Library of Congress** Includes poetry readings in its cultural programs held in the Coolidge Auditorium, Jefferson Building. Consult the calendar of events or call 287-5000.

# PRINTS AND POSTERS

**Capitol Hill Art and Frame Co.** 623 Pennsylvania Avenue, S.E. (Capitol Hill); 546-2700. Large collection theater and art exhibition posters.

**Foliograph Gallery** 1821 K Street, N.W. (downtown); 296-8398. Artist show posters; fine art reproductions; theater, movie, and dance playbills; and contemporary graphics.

**Movie Madness** 1635 Wisconsin Avenue, N.W. (Georgetown); 337-7064. Posters from recent and classic films, including fantasy and science fiction films. Also dolls, postcards, and film props, etc. Framing service.

**P & C Art, Inc.** 2400 Wisconsin Avenue, N.W. (Georgetown); 965-2485. Original lithographs, prints, art posters.

# RACETRACKS

The Gold Line bus company has very accommodating service to all the racetracks in the area. Their schedules vary during the seasons; call 479-5900 or 488-7016. Racing seasons vary.

**Bowie Race Course** Bowie, Maryland. Toll-free from D.C., 262-8111. Day thoroughbred racing. Post-time, 1 PM. From Washington, use New York Avenue to Route 50 to Route 3 to Route 450. Turn right on Racetrack Road and follow signs.

**Charles Town Race Course** Charles Town, West Virginia. Washington-area telephone: 737-2323. Night thoroughbred racing. Enclosed restaurant; make reservations. Take Route 270 N to Frederick, Maryland; then turn west onto Route 340 to Charles Town and the race track.

**Laurel Race Course** Laurel, Maryland. Office: 301/725-0400. Stable: 301/725-0402. Day thoroughbred racing. Dining room; make reservations.

**Pimlico Race Course** Baltimore, Maryland. 301/542-9400. Day thoroughbred racing. Preakness mid-May. Dining room; make reservations. Take Highway 95 north toward Baltimore to Beltway 695 toward Towson; exit 18 east toward Lochearn. Go about 1½ miles to Northern Parkway and turn left. Go through

3 traffic lights and follow the signs to the right to Pimlico.

**Rosecroft Raceway** 6336 Rosecroft Drive, Oxon Hill, Maryland; 301/567-4000. Dinner reservations: 301/567-4045. Night trotters.

**Timonium Race Course** Timonium, Maryland. 301/252-0200. Day thoroughbred racing.

# RADIO STATIONS

See INFORMATION.

# RAILROADS

See TRANSPORTATION.

# RECORDS AND TAPES

A few of the many record shops are:

**Library of Congress** Sells recordings of folk music, ballads, dances, instrumental pieces, and folk tales from the United States and other countries. A free catalogue of the selections is available upon request from the Recording Laboratory, Library of Congress, Washington, D.C. 20540. Records and tapes are sold by mail or through the gift shops. See SIGHTS WORTH SEEING—GOVERNMENT IN ACTION.

**Olsson's Books & Records** 1239 Wisconsin Avenue, N.W. (Georgetown); 338-6712. Also at 19th and L Streets, N.W. (downtown); 785-5037, and at 1340 Connecticut Avenue, N.W. (Dupont Circle); 785-2662. Complete selection; mail and phone orders.

**Serenade Record Shop** 1800 M Street, N.W. (downtown); 452-0075. Also at 1713 G Street, N.W. (downtown); 638-6648, and at 1710 Pennsylvania Avenue, N.W. (downtown); 638-5580. Complete selection; mail and phone orders.

**Tower Records** 2000 Pennsylvania Avenue, N.W. (Mall, entrance on 21st Street between G and H Streets); 331-2400. Open 9 AM to midnight daily.

# RELIGIOUS SERVICES

Consult the "Religion" section of Saturday's edition of the *Washington Post* newspaper for a list of Washington's churches, temples, and mosques and times of services. Also consult the D.C. Yellow Pages.

If you are seeking information on services in a foreign language, consult the appropriate embassy. A few of the churches with services in a foreign language are included below:

**St. Francis Polish National Catholic Church** 439-8877. Polish and English service every Sunday at 11 AM in the Bethlehem Chapel of the Washington Cathedral, Massachusetts and Wisconsin Avenues, N.W.

**St. John's Church Lafayette Square** 1525 H Street, N.W. (across from the White House); 347-8766. French service every Sunday at 4 PM (There is also a marvelous French lunch served here every Wednesday from noon to 1 PM for about $5.)

**United Church** 1920 G Street, N.W. (downtown); 331-1495. German service the first Sunday of every month at 9:30 AM.

**Washington National Cathedral** Massachusetts and Wisconsin Avenues, N.W.; 537-6200. Weekday and Saturday services at 7:30 AM (Bethlehem Chapel), 12 noon (War Memorial), 4 PM (location varies, consult Cathedral aide wearing purple). Sunday services at 8 AM (Holy Communion, St. Mary's Chapel), 9 AM (Holy Eucharist, Bethlehem Chapel), 10 AM mid-September to mid-June (Folk Eucharist, St. Joseph's Chapel), 11 AM (Holy Eucharist, Main Floor), 4 PM (Evensong, Main Floor). For other information about the Cathedral, see listing under SIGHTS WORTH SEEING—OTHER SIGHTS; MUSIC.

# RESTAURANTS

Two popular restaurant critics in the Washington area are Phyllis Richman for the *Washington Post*, whose guide is published in September in one Sunday's "Washington Post Magazine," and Robert Shoffner for the *Washingtonian*, whose guide is published in January. Below are a few of the restaurants located in the main areas of the city. For a supplemental list, consult the Washington Convention and Visitors Association's *Guide to Dining* (see INFORMATION). See also BOOKS—GUIDES TO WASHINGTON.

The following 12 Blue-Ribbon Award restaurants located in the heart of Washington were chosen by the *Washingtonian's* Robert Shoffner in January 1986.

Cantina d'Italia (***)
China Inn (***)
El Caribe & El Caribe Georgetown (***)
Galileo (***)
La Colline (***)
Le Gaulois (***)
Le Lion d'Or (****)
Le Pavillon (****)
Mel Krupin's (***)
Morton's of Chicago (***)
Szechuan (****)
Vincenzo (***)

Because this list is published annually in January, it consists of restaurants visited in the previous year. All of those listed above have maintained their reputation. The Blue Ribbon Awards signify that the restaurant is superior (***), meaning one of the best of its kind in the area, or excellent (****), meaning the restaurant compares favorably with the best in the country. The January issue actually lists 50 very best restaurants in the Washington area, rated excellent, superior, very good, and good.

Make reservations unless otherwise noted. Lunch generally starts around 11:30 and dinner at 5:30; closing time is about 11 PM unless noted; "open late" means until 1, 2, or 3 AM. Major credit cards accepted unless noted. Fixed-price (*prix-fixe*) menus are available at many formal restaurants, so inquire when making reservations, because some restaurants offer these menus only at early and/or late hours.

Prices in parentheses indicate the lowest and highest price for dinner entrees; entrees for lunch are usually lower priced.

**The African Room** 3102 Mt. Pleasant Street, N.W.; 234-1600. Spicy hot authentic African cuisine. On

Friday and Saturday nights beginning around 10:30, disco dancing. Closed Monday. No credit cards. ($6–12)

**American Cafe** 1211 Wisconsin Avenue, N.W. (Georgetown); 337-3600/no reservations. Open late. Ribs, mesquite-grilled fish and chicken, lobster pie, and soups, sandwiches, desserts. Also at 227 Massachusetts Avenue, N.E. (Capitol Hill); 547-8500. Brunch Sunday. Outdoor cafe. And at 5252 Wisconsin Avenue, N.W.; 363-5400. A market-cafe is located in The Shops at National Place, 13th and F Streets, N.W.; 737-5153. ($6–13)

**Anna Maria's** 1737 Connecticut Avenue, N.W. (Dupont Circle); 667-1444. Italian, pasta and veal. Open late—'til 4 AM Monday–Saturday and 'til 2 AM Sunday—and dancing nightly. ($9–12)

**Armadillo** 4912 Wisconsin Avenue, N.W. (Friendship Heights); 244–3961. Mexican specialties. Sunday brunch. ($5–8)

**Astor** 1813 M Street, N.W. (downtown); 331-7994. Greek; baked eggplant and stuffed vegetables. One dining room has belly dancers. (Restaurant, $4–10; nightclub, $6–13)

**Au Pied de Cochon** 1335 Wisconsin Avenue, N.W. (Georgetown); 333-5440/no reservations. French bistro serving crepes, steamed lobster, and daily specials. Very busy and noisy; open 24 hours. ($5–10)

**Aux Beaux Champs** Four Seasons Hotel, 2800 Pennsylvania Avenue, N.W. (Georgetown); 342-0444. French; fancy. Saturday and Sunday brunch. Opens early for breakfast. ($25–55)

**Aux Fruits de Mer** 1329 Wisconsin Avenue, N.W.; 965-2377/no reservations. French; serving seafood. Open late. Brunch Saturday and Sunday. ($8–14)

**A.V. Ristorante** 607 New York Avenue, N.W.; 737-0550. Since 1949, has been serving a broad selection of Italian cuisine, from white pizza to daily seasonal specials such as conch salad. Relaxed atmosphere including oilcloth-covered tables. Closed Sunday. ($5–14)

**Bacchus** 1827 Jefferson Place, N.W. (downtown); 785-0734. Middle Eastern; appetizers, kebabs. Closed Sunday. ($8–12)

**Bamiyan** 3320 M Street, N.W. (Georgetown); 338-1896. Afghan; aushak. Dinner only; closed Sunday. ($7–14)

**Bistro Français** 3124–28 M Street, N.W. (Georgetown); 338-3830. French; roasted chicken and fish. Champagne brunch on Saturday and Sunday. ($9–13)

**Blues Alley** No. 1 Blues Alley (rear 1073 Wisconsin Avenue, Georgetown); 337-4141. Jazz club serving dinner, mainly Creole. Internationally known jazz musicians. ($10–17)

**Booeymonger** 5252 Wisconsin Avenue, N.W. (near Friendship Heights Metro); 686-5805. Also at 3265 Prospect Street, N.W. (Georgetown); 333-4810. Freshly prepared overstuffed sandwiches, salads big enough for a meal, and whole range of desserts including fresh fruit. Open for breakfast 'til late evening daily. No credit cards. ($3–5)

**Bootsie, Winkey and Miss Maud** 2026 P Street, N.W.; 887-0900. Small intimate restaurant serving American cuisine with French flavor. Lunch and dinner daily, except Saturday and Sunday, dinner only. (Lunch and dinner, $5–13)

**Bread & Chocolate** 5542 Connecticut Avenue, N.W. (near Chevy Chase Circle); 966-7413/no reservations. Famous for baked breads; soup, sandwich, salad, and dessert menu. Open for breakfast 'til late evening. ($4–8)

**Bridge Street Cafe** 3116 M Street, N.W. (Georgetown); 342-1854. Light-fare dinner menu featuring seafood, chicken, beef, and large salads. Garden dining offered. Lunch and dinner, Monday–Sunday; Sunday brunch. ($9–12)

**Cafe Mozart** 1331 H Street, N.W. (Metro Center, 13th Street exit, or MacPherson Square Metro stop); 347-5732. German and Viennese cuisine specializing in veal schnitzels, German sausages, and salads. Live entertainment each evening, such as trios, quartets, or pianists, playing classical and popular tunes. Breakfast, lunch, and dinner daily. ($5–15)

**Cafe Rabelais** 1647 Connecticut Avenue, N.W. (Dupont Circle Metro stop); no phone! A popular spot to catch the passing scene only on warm days. Open 11:30 AM 'til late or early the next morning. 15% tip added to tab; cash only. ($5–9)

**Cafe Splendide** 1521 Connecticut Avenue, N.W.; 328-1503. Austrian/Hungarian. Dining in the outdoor garden, from 1514 19th Street, N.W. Breakfast, lunch, and dinner. No credit cards. ($5–10)

**Calvert Restaurant** 1967 Calvert Street, N.W. (Adams Morgan); 232-5431. Middle Eastern; everything is delicious. Belly dancing and live music Wednesday through Saturday, 10 PM. No credit cards. ($5–8)

**Cantina d'Italia•••** 1214A 18th Street, N.W. (Dupont Circle); 659–1830/no reservations required. Northern Italian; homemade pasta and everything else. Numerous awards. Closed Saturday, Sunday and legal holidays. (Lunch, $13–20; dinner, $15–25)

**Chardonnay** In the Park Terrace Hotel, 1515 Rhode Island Avenue, N.W. (Dupont Circle Metro stop, Circle exit); 232-7000. New American cuisine. Breakfast, lunch, and dinner daily, and Sunday brunch. (Dinner $15–27; lunch entrees half that)

**Charing Cross** 3027 M Street, N.W. (Georgetown); 338-2141/if 5 or more for dinner, make reservations. Italian; pasta. ($6–11)

**Charlie Chiang's** 1912 I Street, N.W.; 293-6000. "New-style" Chinese restaurant serving Hunan and Sichuan cuisine. Outdoor dining. Valet parking at dinnertime. Near Farragut West Metro stop. Also at Van Ness Center, 4250 Connecticut Avenue, N.W. (Van Ness Metro stop); 966-1916. ($9–11)

**Chez Artiste** 1201 Pennsylvania Avenue, N.W. (Metro Center or Federal Triangle Metro stops); 737-7772. French and American cuisine in pleasant atmosphere convenient to sights along Pennsylvania Avenue and The Mall. Breakfast Monday–Friday from 7:30 AM; Sunday champagne brunch. Supperclub in the evening (see NIGHTLIFE). Carryout service. ($14–18)

**Chez Grand Mere** 3057 M Street, N.W. (Georgetown); 337-2436. French country cooking. Closed Monday and for lunch on Saturday. ($3–15)

**Chez Odette** 3063 M Street, N.W. (Georgetown); 333-9490. Small, very pleasant restaurant serving Northern Italian cuisine with daily specials. ($11–18)

**Childe Harrold** 1610 20th Street, N.W.; 483-6700. Pleasant dining room with quiet music; serving fresh seafood, steaks, veal, hamburgers, and salads. Bar with jukebox playing country/western and popular rock and roll. Sidewalk patio dining, weather permitting. Sunday brunch. ($7.50–13)

**China Inn•••** 629–631 H Street, N.W.; 842-0909. Established 1937. Authentic Cantonese food. Award winner. Open late. ($7–15)

**Churreria Madrid** 2505 Champlain Street, N.W. (Adams Morgan); 483-4441. Spanish; homemade soups and churros. Closed Monday. ($4–9)

**City Lites** 3025 Prospect Street, N.W. (Georgetown); 333-5483 (333-LITE). Vitamins, diet aids, cosmetics, *and* cafe, market, and carryout selling healthful, very special food. Open daily. ($3–5)

**Clyde's** 3236 M Street, N.W. (Georgetown); 333-0294. American pub, omelet room, and atrium. Serving hamburgers, pasta, seafood, etc. Open late. Breakfast Monday–Friday 7:30–11; brunch Saturday, 10 AM; Sunday, 9 AM. ($6–15)

**Crawdaddy** 539 8th Street, S.E. (Eastern Market Metro stop); 546-7766. Cajun, Creole, and American specialties. Lunch and dinner, and brunch on Saturday and Sunday. Complimentary valet parking Monday–Saturday. ($10–18)

**Csiko's** 3601 Connecticut Avenue, N.W. (uptown in the Broadmoor Apartments); 362-5624. Hungarian; roast duck. Dinner only. Closed Sunday. ($9–12)

**Dominique's** 1900 Pennsylvania Avenue, N.W., corner of 20th Street and Pennsylvania Avenue (downtown); 452-1126. French; everything is perfect. Popular pre- and post-theater prix-fixe dinners ($13). Closed Sunday. ($15–25)

**Duke Zeibert's** Washington Square at 1050 Connecticut Avenue, N.W.; 466-3730. An old Washington favorite specializing in American and Continental cuisine. Closed Sundays during July and August. ($14–20)

**El Bodegon** 1637 R Street, N.W. (Dupont Circle); 667-1710. Iberian Spanish; squid. Flamenco dancer nightly. Separate barroom. Closed Sunday. ($8–15)

**El Caribe\*\*\*** 3288 M Street, N.W. (Georgetown); 338-3121. Also at 1828 Columbia Road, N.W. (Adams Morgan); 234-6969. Latin American cuisine and award winner. Music. ($9–14)

**Enriqueta's** 2811 M Street, N.W. (Georgetown); 338-7772. Mexican; way above Tex-Mex. Weekends, dinner only. ($8–12)

**F. Scott's** 1232 36th Street, N.W. (Georgetown); 965-1789. Supper club with Northern Italian and Continental menu. Special frozen drinks. Dancing. Open late. *Esquire* said this had one of the 4 best bars in Washington. ($12–17)

**Restaurants**

**Fio's** 3636 16th Street, N.W. (uptown, in the Woodner Apartments); 667-3040. Southern Italian; daily specials. Dinner only. Closed Monday. ($4–10)

**Fishery** 5511 Connecticut Avenue, N.W. (uptown); 363-2144. Outdoor dining. American; seafood. ($12–19)

**Floriana** 4936 Wisconsin Avenue, N.W.; 362-9009. Generous appetizers; pasta and veal dishes are favorites. On Saturday, dinner only. Closed Sunday. ($8–15)

**Florida Avenue Grill** 1100 Florida Avenue, N.W. (downtown); 265-1586/no reservations. Popular place with good reviews, serving Southern American soul food. Breakfast from 6 AM. No credit cards; no alcoholic beverages. Closed Sunday. ($4–8)

**Foggy Bottom Cafe** 924 25th Street, N.W. (in the River Inn, near Foggy Bottom Metro stop); 338-8707. American. Breakfast daily. Popular place for performers after their shows at the Kennedy Center. ($8–15)

**Foundry Restaurant** 1050 30th Street, N.W. (Georgetown); 337-1500. American; seafood, steaks, and pasta. Sunday brunch. ($8–17)

**Four Ways Restaurant** 1701 20th Street, N.W. between Connecticut Avenue and R Street (Dupont Circle North Metro stop); 483-3200. French and Continental nouvelle cuisine. This restaurant is in the Fraser Mansion, *c.* 1890 (16 fireplaces). Closed for lunch on Saturday. Sunday brunch. Free valet parking. ($19–22)

**Galileo***** 2014 P Street, N.W. (Dupont Circle Metro stop); 293-7191. An Italian restaurant with a sensitive, creative kitchen. ($10–16)

**Garden Terrace** Four Seasons Hotel, 2800 Pennsylvania Avenue, N.W. (Georgetown); 342-0444/no reservations. Salad and sandwich plates. Open air or sunny windows. Afternoon tea daily from 3–4:30. Open late. ($6–15)

**Geppetto** 2917 M Street, N.W. (Georgetown); 333-2602/no reservations. Italian; antipasto and Sicilian pizza. Dinner only on Sunday. ($8–12)

**Germaine's** 2400 Wisconsin Avenue, N.W. (Georgetown); 965-1185. Oriental cuisine; daily specials and whole fish. Dinner only on Saturday and Sunday. ($10–25)

**Glorious Cafe** 3251 Prospect Street, N.W. (Georgetown in Georgetown Court); 342-0666. Serving New

American and French dishes for lunch and dinner daily. Specials include soups, salads, pizzas, pastas, and omelettes. Regular items include steaks, burgers, and fresh seafood. Especially nice outdoor dining in an unusually large and attractively landscaped garden, weather permitting. Brunch Sunday. (Lunch and dinner, $8–16)

**Golden Palace** 726 7th Street, N.W. (downtown, Chinatown); 783-1225. Cantonese, Hunan, and Szechuan cuisine. ($5–10)

**Harvey's** 1001 18th Street, N.W. (downtown); 833-1858. American; local seafood. On Saturday and Sunday, dinner only. Closed Sunday during summer. ($14–27)

**Houston's** 1065 Wisconsin Avenue, N.W. (Georgetown); 338-7760. American cuisine featuring fresh fish and steak. Closed Sunday. ($6–14)

**Huddle Coffee Shop** 1625 I Street, N.W.; 331-1515. Specialty is Tunisian chicken couscous made daily. Monday–Friday, 11–4. No credit cards. ($3–5)

**Inter-High Connection Restaurant** 2406 18th Street, N.W. (Adams Morgan); 232-8080. American cuisine for breakfast, lunch, and dinner, Monday–Saturday; closed Sunday. Other services include carryout, catering, party-room rentals, discount gift coupons, and 10% discount to seniors and to college and D.C. public school students with ID. Operated by the D.C. Public Schools. ($4–7)

**Intrigue** 824 New Hampshire Avenue, N.W.; 333-2266. English club atmosphere; varied menu. Near the State Department and Kennedy Center and Foggy Bottom Metro stop. Closed Sunday. Popular place for performers after their shows at the Kennedy Center. ($9–17)

**Iron Gate Inn** 1734 N Street, N.W. (Dupont Circle); 737-1370. Middle Eastern; stuffed vegetables, kibbeh, and desserts. Garden open in season. ($8–14)

**Japan Inn** 1715 Wisconsin Avenue, N.W.; 337-3400. Tepanyaki grills, sushi bar, and tatami rooms. ($10–20)

**Jean Jacques Fournil** 1220 19th Street, N.W. (Dupont Circle Metro stop, N Street exit); 466-4264. French, specializing in breads; specials of the day. Breakfast weekdays from 8 AM; brunch on Saturday. Closed Sunday. ($8–13)

**Jockey Club** at the Ritz-Carlton Hotel, 2100 Massachusetts Avenue, N.W.; 659-8000. Famous warm and comforting dining room, serving French continental breakfast, lunch, and dinner daily; Sunday brunch. Free valet parking. ($18–25)

**Joe and Mo's** 1211 Connecticut Avenue, N.W. (downtown); 659-1211. American steakhouse; best of its kind in town—very popular. Breakfast, weekdays; Saturday, dinner only. Closed Sunday. ($12–24)

**Kalorama Cafe** 2228 18th Street, N.W. (Adams Morgan); 667-1022/reservations for 5 or more. Fresh, natural, homemade foods; specializing in pasta, seafood, and pizza. Sunday brunch. Outdoor dining. Closed Sunday night and Monday. No credit cards. ($6–9)

**Kelly's Country Living** 4849 Massachusetts Avenue, N.W. (Spring Valley); 265-1586. Light French menu. Restaurant is within a nice shop selling kitchenware and linens. ($9–11)

**Khyber Pass** 2309 Calvert Street, N.W. (uptown); 234-4632. Afghan; aushak. Dinner only on weekends. ($7–11)

**La Brasserie** 239 Massachusetts Avenue, N.E. (Capitol Hill); 546-9154. French; fish and veal. Sunday brunch. Outdoor dining. ($7–16)

**La Casita of Capitol Hill** 723 8th Street, S.E.; 543-9022. Mexican; everything homemade. ($7–12)

**La Chaumiere** 2813 M Street, N.W. (Georgetown); 338-1784. French country inn. On Saturday, dinner only; closed Sunday. ($9–18)

**La Colline\*\*\*** 400 N. Capitol Street, N.W.; 737-0400. The *Washingtonian* says this is by far the best place to eat on Capitol Hill. French specialties, some Creole inspired. Bouillabaisse is highly recommended. Monday–Friday, for breakfast, lunch, and dinner; weekends, dinner only. ($8–15)

**Lafitte** 1310 New Hampshire Avenue, N.W., in the Hampshire Hotel (downtown); 466-7978. Cajun and Creole specialties. Saturday, dinner only. Sunday brunch. ($9–21)

**La Ruche** 1039 31st Street, N.W. (Georgetown); 965-2684/no reservations. French; daily specials. Garden Sunday brunch. ($6–12)

**Le Gaulois\*\*\*** 2133 Pennsylvania Avenue, N.W. (downtown); 466-3232. French. Extremely popular. Outdoor dining. On Saturday, dinner only; closed Sunday. ($9–15)

**Le Lion D'Or****** 1150 Connecticut Avenue, N.W. (downtown); 296-7972. French; award winner. On Saturday, dinner only; closed Sunday. ($20–28)

**Le Pavillon****** Washington Square at Connecticut Avenue and L Street, N.W.; 833-3846. French; award winner. Closed Sunday. ($23–26; and 2 prix-fixe menus)

**Madurai Vegetarian Restaurant** 3318 M Street, N.W.; 333-0997. Dosai and uthappan are favorites; also curries and desserts. On Sundays there is an "all you can eat" buffet for $6.95. ($4–7)

**Maison Blanche** 1725 F Street, N.W. (downtown); 842-0070. French. Quiet space overlooking ice skaters in the winter. On Saturday, dinner only; closed Sunday. ($16–24)

**Market House** 3276 M Street, N.W. (Georgetown). Food bazaar; here is an array of mini restaurants specializing in pizza; hamburgers; Chinese, German, and Japanese food; seafood (by Cannon's); ice cream; flowers; cheeses, etc. Market House opens at 10 AM and closes about 9 PM. Closed Sunday. No reservations; no credit cards. ($2–7)

**Market Inn** 200 E Street, S.W. (Southwest); 554-2100. Seafood; Maine lobster. Open late. Extensive menu of 85 items. Outdoor dining. ($8–15)

**Martin's Tavern** 1264 Wisconsin Avenue, N.W. (Georgetown); 333-7370. American; raw bar, fresh seafood and seafood salads, prime rib, pan-fried chicken, sandwiches. Since 1933. Open for breakfast at 8 AM daily. ($4–16)

**Mel Krupin's*** 1120 Connecticut Avenue, N.W. (downtown); 331-7000. American; boiled beef and boiled chicken with matzo balls; crab cakes. Closed Sunday. Music. ($14–21)

**Mikado** 4707 Wisconsin Avenue, N.W. (uptown); 244-1740. Japanese. Peaceful and authentic; full-course meals run $12 and up but plenty to choose from for far less. On Sunday, dinner only; closed Monday. ($8–13)

**Moghal Mahal** 2623 Connecticut Avenue at Calvert Street, N.W.; 483-1115. Specializing in Indian cuisine. ($6–12)

**Monsieur Croissant** 1725 K Street, N.W.; 775-9193. Bakery and restaurant. Monday–Friday, breakfast through dinner, closing at 7 PM. Saturday, 10–5. Closed Sunday. ($3–7)

**Restaurants**

**Montpelier Room** Madison Hotel, 15th and M Streets, N.W. (downtown); 862-1712. Continental. Service is tops. On Saturday, dinner only; Sunday brunch. ($17–22)

**Morton's of Chicago***** 3251 Prospect Street, N.W., in Georgetown Court; 342-6258. (Reservations not accepted for seating after 7 PM.) Perfectly timed prime steaks; also lobster and veal. Dinner only, Monday–Saturday. ($11–20)

**Mr. K's** 2121 K Street, N.W.; 331-8868. The best traditional Chinese cuisine. Valet parking at dinnertime. ($8–25)

**Mr. L's** 5018 Connecticut Avenue, N.W.; 244-4343. Jewish-style deli and Chinese cuisine. Open for breakfast daily. ($4–12)

**Mr. M's** 1120 Connecticut Avenue, N.W. (downtown in the lobby of the Bender Building, next to Mel Krupin's); 331-7005. Daily specials, sandwiches, and milk shakes from Mel Krupin's kitchen at half the price. No alcoholic drinks. No credit cards. Monday–Friday, 7:30 AM–4 PM. ($3–7)

**National Gallery Cafeteria & 3 Cafes** National Gallery of Art, 6th Street and Constitution Avenue, N.W. (on the Mall); 347-9401/no reservations. American beer and wine only. Cafeteria and Cascade Cafe on the Concourse; Terrace Cafe in the East Building; and Garden Cafe in the West Building. No credit cards.

**New Orleans Cafe** 1790 Columbia Road, N.W. (Adams Morgan); 234–5111/no reservations. Cajun and Creole food. Serving breakfast, lunch, and dinner daily. ($4–13)

**New Orleans Emporium** 2477 18th Street, N.W. (Adams Morgan); 328–3421. Cajun and Creole seafood. Brunch Saturday and Sunday. ($12–19)

**Old Ebbitt Grill** 675 15th Street, N.W. (downtown); 347-4800. American bar and grill in historic atmosphere. Breakfast Monday–Saturday; Sunday brunch at 10 AM. Sandwiches also served in the evening until 1 AM. ($6–15)

**Old Europe** 2434 Wisconsin Avenue, N.W. (Georgetown); 333-7600. Popular German cuisine; cheesecake and other dessert specialties. Live music nightly. Rathskeller open Friday and Saturday evening. ($9–16)

**Omega** 1858 Columbia Road, N.W. (Adams Morgan); 462-1732. Spanish and Latin American. Plain and very popular. Closed Monday. ($7–11)

**Paru's Indian Vegetarian Restaurant** 2010 S Street, N.W. (Dupont Circle); 483-5133/no reservations. Small and very plain; food is nicely filling. Closes at 9:30 PM; closed Sunday. No credit cards. No alcoholic beverages. ($3–8)

**Patent Pending** At the National Museum of American Art and the National Portrait Gallery, 9th and G Streets, N.W. (downtown); 638-6503/no reservations. American; homemade soups and sandwiches; beer and wine only. Breakfast from 8 AM to 10:30 AM; closes at 3:30 daily and on weekends at 4. ($3–5)

**Phillip's Flagship** 900 Water Street, S.W.; 488-8515. One of the few opportunities to dine on seafood outdoors on the waterfront. A large, very popular restaurant. ($7–19)

**Powerscourt** 520 North Capitol Street (in the Phoenix Park Hotel, Union Station Metro stop); 737-3776. Elegant Irish restaurant. Saturday, dinner only; closed Sunday. ($13–19)

**Red Sea** 2463 18th Street, N.W.; 483-5000. Authentic Ethiopian cuisine. Bar. Open late every night and until 3 AM on Friday. ($4–8)

**Restaurant Nora's** 2132 Florida Avenue, N.W. (downtown); 462-5143. American; fresh and imaginative. Saturday, dinner only; closed Sunday. No credit cards but personal check will be accepted. ($9–17)

**Roma** 3419 Connecticut Avenue, N.W.; 363-6611. Italian-American cuisine since 1920. Delightful garden dining under the grape arbor. Daily 11 AM–1 AM. Violinist and pianist perform Wednesday through Saturday, 7–11 PM. ($9–13)

**Roof Terrace** At the John F. Kennedy Center, 2700 F Street, N.W. (Foggy Bottom); 833-8870. Continental. View of the setting sun and the Potomac River. Sunday brunch. ($12–17)

**Ruth's Chris Steak House** 1801 Connecticut Avenue, N.W., at S Street; 797-0033. Famous in America for great aged U.S. prime steaks. Generally, dinner only. ($16–19)

**Shezan** 913 19th Street, N.W. (downtown); 659-5555. Pakistani; tandoori chicken and lamb kebab. On Saturday, dinner only; closed Sunday. ($5–15)

**Shiroya** 2423 Pennsylvania Avenue, N.W.; 887-9507. Sushi, sashimi, sukiyaki, and tempura. Saturday, dinner only; closed Sunday. ($8–15)

**Sholl's Cafeteria** 1990 K Street, N.W. (downtown in the Esplanade Mall); 296-3065/no reservations. Very popular, and the lines move fast. Breakfast begins at 7 AM Monday–Saturday; cafeteria closes at 8 PM; closed Sunday. No credit cards. No alcoholic beverages. ($3–5)

**Sichuan Garden** 1220 19th Street, N.W. between M and N Streets (Dupont Circle Metro stop); 296-4550. Authentic Sichuan cuisine directly from the Sichuan (Chongqing) Province by the People's Republic of China—first restaurant of its kind in the United States. Seven vegetable entrees to choose from as well as meat, chicken, and seafood entrees. Lunch and dinner (closed from 3:30 to 5:30 PM). Valet parking after 5:30. ($6–25)

**Sushiko** 2309 Wisconsin Avenue, N.W. (North Georgetown); 333-4187. Japanese; sushi bar and dining room. On Saturday and Sunday, dinner only; closed Monday. ($4–13)

**Suzanne's** 1735 Connecticut Avenue, N.W. (Dupont Circle); 483-4633/no reservations. Upstairs from her carryout; wine bar and casual menu. Closed Sunday. ($9–14)

**Szechuan····** 615 I Street, N.W. (downtown/Chinatown); 393-0131. Szechuan-Hunan specialties; excellent reviews; award winner. Dim Sum or brunch on Saturday and Sunday. ($7–15)

**Tabard Inn** 1739 N Street, N.W. (Dupont Circle); 785-1277/reservations for dinner or for lunch with 6 or more. Daily specials are inventive. Garden open in season for drinks and for very light hors d'oeuvres in the evening. *Esquire* said here was one of Washington's 4 best bars. Visa and Mastercard only. Open for breakfast. ($8–12)

**Tandoor···** 3316 M Street, N.W. (Georgetown); 333-3376. Indian; soup, chicken, vegetable curry. Award winner. ($6–12)

**Taverna the Greek Islands** 307 Pennsylvania Avenue, S.E.; 547-8360. Sampler plate and lamb dishes are favorites. On Sunday, dinner only. ($4–13)

**Thai Room** 5037 Connecticut Avenue, N.W. (uptown); 244-5933. Excellent but watch the fiery seasoning. ($5–15)

**Thai Taste** 2606 Connecticut Avenue, N.W., near Calvert Street (Woodley Park Metro stop); 387-8876.

Lightly spiced Thai cuisine in Art Deco atmosphere. Sunday, dinner only. ($4–13)

**The Buck Stops Here** 17th and G Streets, N.W. (Liberty Plaza, downtown); 842-0227. No reservations. Cafeteria. 6:45 AM to 2:30 PM, Monday–Friday. ($2–6)

**Timberlake's** 1726 Connecticut Avenue, N.W. (Dupont Circle); 483-2266/no reservations. Bar/restaurant serving American menu of good sandwiches, salads, quiches, etc., with dining in the sunroom. Jukebox with wide range of soul, R&B, and top 40. Saturday and Sunday brunch. Open late. (Sandwich menu, $5–7; dinner menu, $7–12)

**Tout Va Bien** 1063 31st Street, N.W.; 965-1212. Highly recommended are the soupe a l'oignon, vegetable terrine, and fish dishes. Dinner only on Sunday. ($9–15)

**Tunnicliffs Tavern** 222 7th Street, S.E.; 546-3663. Mesquite grilling. Outdoor cafe, weather permitting. Saturday breakfast and Sunday brunch. ($8–12)

**Vie de France Cafe** 600 Maryland Avenue, S.E.; 554-7870. Also at 4250 Connecticut Avenue, N.W. in the Van Ness Metro station; 364-8888; and at 1990 K Street, N.W. (Esplanade Mall); 659-0055. Also **Fast & Fresh**, 1723 K Street, N.W.; 775–9193. Light meals with freshly baked French flair. Closed Saturday and Sunday. ($2–5)

**Vincenzo\*\*\*** 1606 20th Street, N.W.; 667-0047. Pristine superb Northern Italian seafood. Outdoor dining in season. Lunch Monday–Friday, noon to 2 PM. Dinner Monday–Saturday. Closed Sunday. (Lunch and dinner, $13–18)

**Yenching Palace** 3524 Connecticut Avenue, N.W. (uptown); 362-8200. Chinese; Peking duck. Friday and Saturday open late. ($5–10; Peking duck, $19)

**Zorba's Cafe** 1612 20th Street, N.W. (Dupont Circle Metro stop, Q Street exit); 387-8555/no reservations. Greek and Mediterranean specialties—everything is strictly homemade. Lunch and dinner daily. ($3–6)

## Restaurants in Department Stores

**Greenbrier Room at Garfinckels** 14th and F Streets, N.W. (downtown); 628-7730/no reservations. Lunch, tea, and on Thursday, dinner 'til 7 PM. Cocktails ($3–8)

**Woodward & Lothrop** 11th and F Streets, N.W. (downtown); 347-5300. Woodies has numerous restaurants including fast-food, cafeteria, pub, and dining room. Cocktails in pub and dining room. ($3–8)

## Restaurants in Museums and in Sights Worth Seeing

**Federal government offices** have cafeterias, most of which are open to the public for breakfast and lunch Monday–Friday. Some of these cafeterias are: Rayburn and Longworth House Office Buildings, Senate Office Building, Library of Congress (James Madison Building), Treasury, Commerce Department, Supreme Court.

**National Gallery of Art** has a cafeteria and 3 cafes.

**National Museum of American Art and National Portrait Gallery** have Patent Pending.

**Smithsonian Museums** (for information call 357-2700): National Museum of American History cafeteria and ice cream parlor; Air & Space Museum, fast-food; Natural History Museum, fast-food and the Associates private restaurant, which is open for breakfast during the summer months—very busy place.

## Restaurants in Shopping Malls

See SHOPPING MALLS AND CENTERS for locations. Shopping malls have a nice selection of restaurants. Especially recommended is the Pavilion at the Old Post Office Building and The Shops at National Place. The large variety of kiosks and restaurants offer everything from french fries to seafood, and from American fare to Indian cuisine.

For addresses of the following restaurants, see the alphabetical listing beginning on page 114.

## Brunch

American Cafe, Armadillo, Aux Beaux Champs, Aux Fruits de Mer, Bistro Français, Bridge Street Cafe, Chardonnay, Clyde's, Crawdaddy, the Foundry, Four

Ways, Glorious Cafe, Jean Jacques Fournil, Jockey Club, Kalorama Cafe, La Brasserie, Lafitte, La Ruche, New Orleans Emporium, Old Ebbitt Grill, Roof Terrace, Szechuan, Timberlake's, Tunnicliffs Tavern.

## Breakfast

Aux Beaux Champs, Booeymonger, Bread & Chocolate, The Buck Stops Here, Cafe Splendide, Chardonnay, Clyde's, Florida Avenue Grill, Foggy Bottom Cafe, Inter-High Connection, Jockey Club, Joe & Mo's, La Colline, Martin's Tavern, Monsieur Croissant, Mr. L's, Mr. M's, Old Ebbitt Grill, Sholl's, Tabard Inn, Tunnicliffs Tavern.

## Live Music

Anna Maria's, Astor, Blues Alley, Calvert Restaurant, Chez Artiste, El Bodegon, F. Scott's, Mel Krupin's, Roma, Timberlake's.

## Open-Air

American Cafe, Bridge Street Cafe, Cafe Rabelais, Cafe Splendide, Charlie Chiang's, Fishery, Garden Terrace, Glorious Cafe, Iron Gate Inn, Kalorama Cafe, La Brasserie, La Ruche, Le Gaulois, Market Inn, Roma, Tabard Inn, Tunnicliffs Tavern, Vincenzo.

## View

Cafeteria of the Library of Congress in the James Madison Building, Maison Blanche, Roof Terrace.

## Open in the Wee Hours of the Morning

American Cafe, Anna Maria's, Au Pied de Cochon, Aux Fruits de Mer, Cafe Rabelais, F. Scott's, Garden Terrace, Market Inn, Red Sea, Timberlake's.

## Cafeterias

National Gallery of Art, the Smithsonian's National Museum of American History, Patent Pending, Scholl's, The Buck Stops Here. See also CARRYOUTS AND DELIS.

## Seafood

Au Pied de Cochon, Aux Fruits de Mer, Fishery, Foundry, Germaine's, Harvey's, La Brasserie, Market Inn, Martin's Tavern, Phillip's Flagship, Vincenzo.

## Steak

Duke Zeibert's, Foundry, Joe & Mo's, Martin's Tavern, Morton's of Chicago, Ruth's Chris Steak House, Tunnicliffs Tavern.

## Natural Foods

City Lites, Madurai Vegetarian Restaurant, Paru's Indian Vegetarian Restaurant.

## Creole

Blues Alley

## Soul

Florida Avenue Grill

## American

American Cafe, Blues Alley, Booeymonger, Bootsie, Winkey & Miss Maud, Bread & Chocolate, Bridge Street Cafe, The Buck Stops Here, Chardonnay, Chez Artiste, Clyde's, Duke Zeibert's, Fishery, Florida Avenue Grill, Foggy Bottom Cafe, Foundry, Garden Terrace, Glorious Cafe, Harvey's, Inter-High Connection, Intrigue, Joe & Mo's, Kalorama Cafe, Kelly's Country

Living, Market House, Market Inn, Mel Krupin's, Morton's of Chicago, Mr. L's, Mr. M's, Old Ebbitt Grill, Patent Pending, Restaurant Nora's, Ruth's Chris Steak House, Sholl's Cafeteria, Suzanne's, Tabard Inn, Timberlake's, Tunnicliffs Tavern.

# Ethnic

**Afghan:** Bamiyan, Khyber Pass.

**African:** African Room.

**Austrian:** Cafe Mozart, Cafe Splendide.

**Cantonese, Hunan, Szechuan:** Charlie Chiang's, China Inn, Golden Palace, Mr. K's, Mr. L's, Sichuan Gardens, Szechuan, Yenching Palace.

**Creole:** Blues Alley, Crawdaddy, Lafitte, New Orleans Cafe, New Orleans Emporium.

**Ethiopian:** Red Sea.

**French:** Au Pied de Cochon, Aux Beaux Champs, Aux Fruits de Mer, Bistro Français, Chez Artiste, Chez Grand Mere, Dominique's, Four Ways, Glorious Cafe, Jean Jacques Fournil, Jockey Club, La Brasserie, La Chaumiere, La Ruche, Le Gaulois, Le Lion d'Or, Le Pavillon, Maison Blanche, Monsieur Croissant, Tout Va Bien, Vie de France Cafe.

**German:** Cafe Mozart, Old Europe.

**Greek:** Aster, Taverna the Greek Islands, Zorba's Cafe.

**Hungarian:** Cafe Splendide, Csiko's.

**Indian:** Madurai Vegetarian, Moghal Mahal, Paru's, Tandoor.

**Irish:** Powerscourt.

**Italian:** Anna Maria's, A.V. Ristorante, Cantina d'Italia, Charing Cross, Chex Odette, F. Scott's, Fio's, Floriana, Galileo, Geppetto, Roma, Vincenzo.

**Japanese:** Japan Inn, Mikado, Shiroya, Sushiko.

**Latin American:** El Caribe, Omega.

**Mexican:** Armadillo, Enriqueta's, La Casita of Capitol Hill.

**Middle Eastern:** Bacchus, Calvert Restaurant, Huddle Coffee Shop, Iron Gate Inn.

**Oriental:** Germaine's.

**Pakistani:** Shezan.

**Soul Food (American):** Florida Avenue Grill.

**Spanish:** Churreria Madrid, El Bodegon, Omega.

**Thai:** Thai Room, Thai Taste.

# RUNNERS' GUIDE

Visitors to Washington wonder how the government can function with so many joggers. It is true that this is a favorite place for keeping physically fit. A few of the beautiful jogging paths are:

**C & O Canal Towpath** Approached from a variety of spots a block or two west of M Street in Georgetown or from Fletcher's Boat House. This flat packed-earth path is equipped with mileposts. Very best path.

**East and West Potomac Park** Paved and laced with beautiful trees but bordered by automobiles and airplanes landing at National Airport.

**The Mall** 2 miles from the Capitol to Lincoln Memorial and much of it is packed earth with pebbles. Scenic.

**The Tidal Basin and Constitution Gardens** Breathtaking when the cherry blossoms are blooming. Some areas are packed earth.

## Races

Watch *Running Times* magazine. Also races are listed in the "Sporting Life" column of the "Weekend" section of Friday's *Washington Post* and are also listed in the *Washingtonian*. A few of the D.C. races and the clubs conducting the race are:

**Washington's Birthday Marathon** In February; D.C. Road Runners, 474-7177.

**D.C. Marathon and 5K Fun Run** In April, through 8 District Wards. Sponsored by D.C. Department of Recreation, 673-7660.

**Hometown Run** 15K and 3K; mid-May. Sponsored by Washington Urban League (see ANNUAL EVENTS), 265-8200.

**Bonne Bell 10K** In May; Washington Runners Unlimited, 354-4835.

**Hecht's Ten Miler** In June; Washington Running Club, 455-0575.

**Hugh Jascourt Anniversary Run** In June; D.C. Road Runners, 474-7177.

**Georgetown 10K** In October; Washington Running Club, 455-0575.

**Marine Corps Marathon** First Sunday in November, always. Second largest in the nation. 433-2854.
**Thanksgiving Run** In November; Washington Running Club, 455-0575.

## Clubs

A few of the many are:
**D.C. Road Runners** One of the oldest and largest running clubs in the area. Periodic meetings, bimonthly newsletters, running hotline, and low fees for weekly races. Conducts a few major annual races. 474-7177.
**National Capital Track Club** A small, closely knit club that enjoys training together. Periodic meetings, newsletters, and weekend runs at the Washington Sailing Marina. 840-9343.
**Washington Runners Unlimited** An all-women running club emphasizing health and safe training. Monthly meetings, with speakers, newsletters, training runs, track workouts, coaching, and annual banquet. 354-4835.
**Washington Running Club** A very competitive club offering monthly meetings, newsletters, coaching, track workouts, group training runs, and long weekend runs. 455-0575.

## Specialty Shop

**Runner's Store** Moss Brown & Co., 1522 Wisconsin Avenue, N.W. at P Street; 965-4350. Running clothes, shoes, and gear. Watch for new addresses in Washington.

# SECONDHAND CLOTHING AND THRIFT SHOPS

For antique clothing, see SPECIALTY SHOPS.
**Amvets** 6101 Georgia Avenue, N.W. (between Rittenhouse and Quackenboes, 2 blocks from Missouri Avenue going north); 291-4013. Everything from furniture to clothes.

**Goodwill Industries** 2200 South Dakota Avenue, N.E. (Capitol Hill); 636-4225. Clothing, housewares, and furniture.

**Thrift Shop** 2622 P Street, N.W.; 338-8714. Nice things for sale for the benefit of various services to children in Washington.

**Value Village** 4618 14th Street, N.W. (between Buchanan and Clinton); 829-5728. Monday–Saturday, 9 AM–8:45 PM. Everything from furniture to clothes.

# SHOES

**Bally of Switzerland** In Washington Square at 1020 or 1022 Connecticut Avenue, N.W.; 429-0604. Elegant shoes and accessories for men and women.

**Bootlegger** 1420 Wisconsin Avenue, N.W. (Georgetown); 333-0373. Also at 1142 Connecticut Avenue, N.W.; 785-2863. Styles for men and women.

**Hess Shoes** Georgetown Park at Wisconsin Avenue and M Street, N.W. Shoes for women, 333-7043; shoes for men, 333-7044.

**Tall Gals Shoes** On The Promenade at L'Enfant Plaza, corner of 7th and D Streets, S.W. (L'Enfant Plaza Metro stop, Promenade exit); 863-0877. Sizes 10–13, narrow and medium widths.

**Tetra Designs** The Pavilion at the Old Post Office Building, 11th Street and Pennsylvania Avenue, N.W.; 682-1032. Women's shoes.

# SHOPPING MALLS AND CENTERS

Everytime you turn around, there is a new mall to visit. A few of them are:

**Connecticut Connection** 1101 Connecticut Avenue, N.W. at L Street, on top of the Farragut North Metro stop. On the Metro level is a popular food bazaar called The Food Works; these fast-food shops open at 7 AM

for breakfast. Charlie's Crab restaurant opens at 11
AM and closes around midnight. Here also are Crabtree
and Evelyn, Merle Norman Cosmetics, Theodore &
Nye (fine jewelry), Cortese Collection (imported wom-
en's clothes and accessories), and Arthur A. Adler
(men's clothing and accessories). The mall opens at 10
AM and closes at 6 PM, Monday through Saturday.
Some stores, because of their location, are open later.

**F Street Plaza** An informal open-air mall with Woodward & Lothrop at the east end at 11th Street, N.W.,
and Garfinckel's at the west end at 14th Street, N.W.
In between are clothing and shoe shops, Reeves Bakery, sandwich shops, fabric store, and Galt & Bros.,
Inc., on 13th Street—the oldest jewelry store in the
United States. On the plaza is TicketPlace, where you
can buy tickets to that day's theater shows at half
price. The U.S. Post Office even has a do-it-yourself
mailing unit here. Also at the west end is the Willard
Inter-Continental Hotel, Washington Hotel and Old
Ebbitt Grill. In between is the lavish National Place,
which includes an inside shopping mall, The Shops,
the J. W. Marriott Hotel, and the National Theater
(see **National Place**, below).

**Georgetown** Georgetown's main thoroughfare, Wisconsin Avenue and M Street, N.W., is lined with nice
restaurants, bars, quick-eats, hotels, and unique clothing and gift shops. There are several enclosed malls,
most of which are located west of M Street. *Georgetown
Court* is a nice selection of shops and restaurants east
of M Street at 3251 Prospect Street. To get around,
hop aboard the new Old Town Trolley for a person-
alized tour (see TOURS).

The fanciest mall is *Georgetown Park* at 3222 M
Street, N.W. There are more than 100 of the world's
finest merchants and restaurateurs. The hours are
Monday–Saturday, 10–9, and Sunday, 12–6. Along
the C&O Canal Towpath to the south of Georgetown
Park is the *Foundry* at 30th Street. The main attraction is the Foundry Restaurant (see RESTAURANTS) and
Chelsea's (see BARS AND PUBS); there is also a movie
theater and Moss Portfolio (gallery). The mall opens
Monday through Saturday at 10 AM and closes at 6 PM;
on Thursday at 9 PM. Some merchants are open Sunday.

Just north of Georgetown is *Market House*, similar
to Boston's Fanueil Hall in miniature. Here is a pot-

pourri of restaurants, serving everything from pizza to oysters on the half shell to ice cream. The entrance is on M Street; it opens at 10 AM and closes at 8 PM daily; closed Sunday.

See the separate entry in this section for *Washington Harbour*, which is located midway between Georgetown and downtown Washington on the Potomac.

**Les Champs at The Watergate** Virginia Avenue and New Hampshire Avenue, N.W., next to the Kennedy Center. Elegant designer shops, restaurants, hotel, bakeries, etc.

**Mazza Gallerie** Wisconsin Avenue, N.W. at Western Avenue on the Maryland line. The main attraction is Neiman-Marcus. There is also a parfumerie, kitchen equipment shop, chocolate shop, ice cream parlor, and many more attractions. This shopping mall is adjacent to movie theaters, and Lord & Taylor; branches of Woodward & Lothrop and Saks Fifth Avenue are just north of this area in Maryland. This area is known as Friendship Heights. A #30 bus traveling west on Pennsylvania Avenue and north on Wisconsin Avenue will take you there.

**National Place and National Press Building** Encompasses the entire block between 13th and 14th Streets, and F Street, N.W. and Pennsylvania Avenue, N.W. It includes 100 shops, restaurants and cafes, the J.W. Marriott Hotel, the National Theater, and the National Press Building, home of the National Press Club. Monday–Saturday, 10 AM–7 PM, Thursday until 9 PM. Sunday noon–6 PM. Cafes open for breakfast, restaurants open late. Metro Center, 13th Street exit.

**The Pavilion, the Old Post Office Building at the Nancy Hanks Center** 12th Street and Pennsylvania Avenue, N.W. The Old Post Office Building was originally dedicated in 1899. It was built in the "Richardson Romanesque" fanciful style with a bell tower and skylight. In 1977 Arthur Cotton Moore began the remodeling design (having won the Government Services Administration's architectural competition).

The bells in the tower are a gift to the United States from the Ditchley Foundation, England. They are based on the 1596 bells in Westminster Abbey that rang during World War II. The atrium is 99 by 184 feet; the skylight is 196 feet above ground; the tower rises to 315 feet, higher than the Statue of Freedom atop the Capitol. From the tower, one has a 360-degree view of the city. The bells will be rung on national holidays and on the opening and closing days of Congress. (See THINGS TO DO.)

The building contains offices of the National Endowments of Arts and Humanities, Institute of Museum Services, and the Advisory Commission on Historic Preservation. The Pavilion of shops, cafés, and restaurants occupies the lower floors, as does the performing arts stage. Restaurants include Blossoms (with raw bar), Fitz, Fox & Brown (Continental menu), and Richard's Seafood. Events on stage are held daily and advertised in "Weekend" on Fridays in the *Washington Post*.

**2000 Pennsylvania Avenue** Between 20th and 21st Streets, N.W. A new address on the edge of the George Washington University campus. The design of the shopping area incorporates architecturally significant townhouses and buildings.

Shops include Devon Bar & Grill, Alcott & Andrews (classic career clothing for women), Williams the Tailor (alterations, custom tailoring, reweaving), Tower Records, Hess Shoes, gift and jewelry boutiques, cafe/restaurant, and ice cream parlor. Parking at 20th Street entrance. Metro: 2 blocks to Farragut West and 3 blocks to Foggy Bottom (Blue and Orange Lines).

**Washington Harbour** 3000 K Street, N.W. (under the Whitehurst Freeway in Georgetown). A brand-new office/retail/residential/restaurant complex on the Potomac River, featuring a unique design and fountain-laden courtyards. Pedestrians should approach from M Street in Georgetown walking west on Thomas Jefferson Street. Eventually pedestrians will have access to this area via a waterfront promenade from Thompson's Boathouse along the Potomac River by Washington Harbour leading to a park which ends at Wisconsin Avenue.

# SIGHTS WORTH SEEING

Washington is one of the most beautiful cities in the world. If your visit is brief, be sure to drive around at night when the monuments, memorials, buildings, and sculptures are lighted. *Washington, The Capital* (see BOOKS—BOOKS ABOUT WASHINGTON) is one of several photo essays that show how dramatic and peaceful this city can be. The section on TOURS contains information on walking tours if you are interested in historic and modern architecture.

*Washington's Attractions*, published by the Washington Convention and Visitors Association, is a handy brochure with information on nearly 100 attractions and a map. (See INFORMATION.)

Of the places listed below, most are open for tours daily and are free unless noted. Most are closed on major holidays; government buildings are closed on federal holidays and weekends. See also MUSEUMS; LIBRARIES.

# Cemeteries and Memorials

**Arlington National Cemetery** Arlington, Virginia; 692-0931. Tomb of the Unknown Soldier, graves of John F. Kennedy, Robert Kennedy, and William Howard Taft. October through March, daily 8–5; April through September, daily 8–7.

**Congressional Cemetery** 1801 E Street, S.E.; 543-0539. Graves of notables including John Philip Sousa, Matthew Brady, Anne Royall, and Elbridge Gerry, signer of the Declaration of Independence and vice-president under Madison. Call for information on walking tour.

**Jefferson Memorial** South bank of the Tidal Basin; 426-6821. Thomas Jefferson was our 3rd president and author of the Declaration of Independence. Open daily 8 AM–midnight; tours lasting 30 minutes from May through Labor Day. Especially dramatic lighted at night (until midnight). Free band concerts summer evenings. (See MUSIC.)

**Lincoln Memorial** West Potomac Park and 23rd Street, N.W.; 426-6841. Abraham Lincoln was our 16th president. For reservations for "Looking Under Lincoln" (exploring the catacombs) call 426-6895. Open daily 8 AM–midnight. Tours last 30 minutes. (Lighted until midnight.)

**Marine Corps Memorial** Arlington, Virginia (on Rt. 50 across from Memorial Bridge). Depicted is the famous flag raising on Iwo Jima (1945).

JEFFERSON MEMORIAL

**Oak Hill Cemetery** 30th and R Streets, N.W. (Georgetown); 337-2835. Among the famous here are Edwin Stanton, Gen. Jessie Reno, R. Adm. Theodorus Bailey (he was the man really responsible for the capture of New Orleans—for details consult the superintendents at the cemetery!). Monday–Friday, 9–4:30.
**Rock Creek Cemetery** Webster and 3rd Streets, N.W. (between New Hampshire Avenue and N. Capitol Street); 829-0585. At the gravesite of Henry Adams'

LINCOLN MEMORIAL

wife is the Augustus St. Gaudens statue, untitled but
popularly referred to as "Grief" or more appropriately,
"The Peace of God." Monday–Friday, 8:30–4:30;
grounds open daily from 8 to sundown. The Smithsonian Associates tour this cemetery several times a
year.
**Vietnam Veterans Memorial** Constitution Gardens at
Henry Bacon Drive and Constitution Avenue near the
Lincoln Memorial. The names of Vietnam veterans

and those missing in action are inscribed in granite on the memorial, and a bronze sculpture portraying 3 young men carrying the weapons of war stands nearby. There is a permanent name directory located at the entrance to the memorial site.

**Washington Monument** (Completed 1884) On the Mall at 15th Street, N.W.; 426-6839. From 550 feet up see a breathtaking view of Washington. The view is very nice from ground-level too, especially at night when the White House, Capitol, and Lincoln and Jefferson Memorials are lighted. Parking area open 8 AM to 11 PM. Daily, 9–5; summer hours, 8–midnight. (Lighted until midnight.) If you are handicapped, let the guides know and you will be moved to the head of the line.

# Government in Action

**Bureau of Engraving and Printing** 14th and C Streets, S.W.; 447-9709. This is the place where money and stamps are made. Tickets issued on a first-come basis for tours Monday–Friday 9 AM–2 PM. Self-conducted tour lasts 25 minutes. Closed legal holidays.

**Department of State** 2201 C Street, N.W., the Diplomatic Entrance; 647-3241. Three tours daily at 9:30, 10:30, and 3:00. Tour lasts 45 minutes; reservations must be made 4 to 6 weeks in advance. Weather permitting and depending on official schedules, tour includes view of Washington from the rooftop terrace and diplomatic reception rooms furnished with American antiques *c.* 1740–1830.

**Federal Bureau of Investigation** 9th Street and Pennsylvania Avenue, N.W.; 324-3447. One-hour guided tours include FBI labs, firearms demonstrations, and brief history. Monday–Friday 9 AM–4:15 PM; closed legal holidays. Since this is a popular tour, it is wise to make reservations. "Congressional" tours, arranged through your congressman or senator, eliminate the need to wait in line.

**Library of Congress** Thomas Jefferson Building (main building), 1st Street and Independence Avenue, S.E., 287-5000, and the James Madison Memorial Building, 101 Independence Avenue, S.E. Exhibit halls open Monday–Friday 8:30 AM–9:30 PM; Saturday, Sunday, and holidays, 8:30 AM–6 PM. John Adams Building, 2nd Street and Independence Avenue, S.E. Exhibit hall open Monday–Friday, 8:30 AM–9:30 PM; Saturday,

8:30 AM–5 PM. Tours begin in the Orientation Theatre, ground floor, Thomas Jefferson Building, every hour on the hour from 9 AM through 4 PM, Monday–Friday. Slide show (18 minutes) begins 8:45 AM and is shown hourly to 8:45 PM.

**The Old Executive Office Building** Located next to the White House, this magnificent Victorian office building was completed in 1888 and is now occupied by the White House staff, Office of the Vice President, and the National Security Council. Tours of the building's spectacular hallways, meeting rooms, and libraries are given by appointment only and need to be made 3–4 weeks in advance. Tours are Saturday, 9 AM–noon. Call the tour office Monday–Friday, 9–12, 395-5895. Your social security number and birth date will be requested.

**The Pentagon** Arlington, Virginia (mailing address: Washington, D.C. 20301). Tour information, 695-1776. Pay parking in the south parking lot or take the Metrorail to the Pentagon Stop. If going by car take Interstate 395 from the 14th Street Bridge and follow signs to the Pentagon. Follow the signs to the Tour Office. (From Metrorail, take the escalator to the top and follow the signs to the tours.) Tours begin at 9 AM and the last tour begins at 3:30 PM Monday–Friday. Closed holidays. The tour lasts about 1 to 1¼ hours and is not particularly suitable for young children.

**United States Capitol** Cornerstone laid by George Washington September 18, 1793. East end of the Mall. Tour information: 225-6827; to call your senator or congressman: 224-3121. Tours from 9 AM to 3:45 PM daily, lasting anywhere from 20 minutes to an hour depending on the volume of tourists visiting the Capitol. Closed Thanksgiving, Christmas, and New Year's. *Locations of Capitol office buildings:* Cannon House Office Building, 1st Street and Independence Avenue, S.E.; Dirksen Senate Office Building, 1st Street and Constitution Avenue, N.E.: Hart Senate Office Building, 2nd Street and Constitution Avenue, N.E.: Longworth House Office Building, Indiana and New Jersey Avenues, S.E.; Rayburn House Office Building, Independence Avenue and South Capitol Street, S.W.

**U.S. Mint** 15th Street and Pennsylvania Avenue, N.W.; 566-5221. Sales of uncirculated coins. Monday–Friday, 9 AM–4 PM. Closed holidays.

THE CAPITAL

**U.S. Postal Service, Philatelic Sales** 475 L'Enfant Plaza, S.W. Any stamp ever produced, if it is still on sale, is available here in plate block positions. If you are a stamp collector, be sure to include this on your visit to Washington. Exhibit area is part of the sales area. If you need information by telephone, you must call Merrifield, Virginia, a local call from Washington: 703/573-5416. Monday–Saturday, 9 AM–5 PM.

**U.S. Supreme Court** Built in 1935. 1st Street and Maryland Avenue, N.E. Tour information, 479-3030. Marshal's Office, 479-3200. Open to the public Monday–Friday, 9–4:30. Closed holidays. Guided tours available when the Court is not sitting. Public sessions begin at 10 AM and continue until 3 PM, with a 1-hour recess at noon. Cafeteria open for breakfast and lunch. Public sessions are not held on Fridays.

**White House** 1600 Pennsylvania Avenuue, N.W.; 456-7041. First inhabited by John and Abigail Adams, 1800. Tours lasting 20 minutes are given Tuesday through Saturday, 10 AM–noon. Entrance for the tour is through the East Gate on East Executive Avenue across from the Treasury Department.

To accommodate the summer tourists from Memorial Day weekend through Labor Day weekend, free color-coded tickets are distributed from the Park Service kiosk beginning at 8 AM for the tour that day. The kiosk is located on the Ellipse near the White House. Tickets must be picked up by each individual visitor on a first-come, first-served basis (426-6700).

Tickets for a more detailed free tour earlier in the morning are distributed by your congressman or senator on a limited basis, so it is wise to write or call his or her office well in advance of your anticipated visit. Closed some holidays for presidential functions; if in doubt, call 456-7041 for confirmation.

## Landmarks and Historic Homes

**Anderson House** 2118 Massachusetts Avenue, N.W. (Dupont Circle Metro stop, Q Street exit); 785-0540. Given to the Society of the Cincinnati (see LIBRARIES) for its headquarters in 1937, this prime example of the Washington "great house," completed in 1906, had been the home of Larz Anderson, Ambassador to Belgium and Japan. Ambassador Anderson's European and Oriental art and antiques are on exhibit, as are

SUPREME COURT BUILDING

the Society's portraits and artifacts pertaining to the American Revolution and George Washington's Continental Army and related material. Concerts, lectures, and other special events are scheduled periodically. Member, Dupont Kalorama Museum Consortium (see MUSEUMS).

**Barney Studio House** 2306 Massachusetts Avenue, N.W. (Dupont Circle Metro stop, Q Street exit); 357-3111. Alice Pike Barney established this studio in her home, the second structure to be built on Sheridan Circle, as a place where people could discuss and share cultural experiences in art and music. Now it is part of the Smithsonian's National Museum of American Art and a member of the Dupont Kalorama Museum Consortium (see MUSEUMS—ART MUSEUMS). Guided visits by reservation. Closed July through September.

**Blair House** 1650 Pennsylvania Avenue, N.W. Across from the Executive Offices of the White House and adjacent to the Renwick Gallery are 3 homes referred to as one: Blair House. They were built c. 1824; two were purchased by the Government in 1942 and the third home was purchased c. 1971. They are used as residences for visiting diplomatic guests of the president. Tours are not given.

**Clara Barton House** 5801 Oxford Road, Glen Echo, Maryland (at MacArthur Boulevard and Goldsboro Road). A National Historic Site. Clara Barton's final home, which served as headquarters for the American Red Cross from 1897 to 1904. The large mid-Victorian house is of unusual design with an interior resembling a Mississippi riverboat. The house, open daily from 10 AM–5 PM, is slowly being changed back to the way it was when Miss Barton lived there. It is located adjacent to the Glen Echo Park (see PARKS AND NATURE PRESERVES).

**Columbia Historical Society/Christian Heurich Mansion** 1307 New Hampshire Avenue, N.W. (Dupont Circle); 785-2068. Built in 1892. Home of the Columbia Historical Society. Tours on Friday and Saturday, noon–4 PM. Member, Dupont Kalorama Museum Consortium (see MUSEUMS—ART MUSEUMS). $1 contribution requested of adult visitors.

**Decatur House** 748 Jackson Place, N.W. (downtown at Lafayette Park); 673-4030. Commodore Stephen Decatur's townhouse, built in 1818. Tuesday–Friday, 10 AM–4 PM; Saturday and Sunday, noon–4 PM. Adults,

$2.50; senior citizens and students, $1.25. Old Town Trolley stops here.

**Ford's Theatre** 511 10th Street, N.W.; 426-6924. On exhibit are a museum and the theater where Abraham Lincoln was shot (theater not shown during matinees). Daily, 9 AM–5 PM; closed Christmas Day. Old Town Trolley stops here. See also THEATERS; TOURS.

**Frederick Douglass Memorial Home** 1411 W Street, S.E.; 426-5960. Douglass (1817–1895) was a slave and became a writer, orator, and diplomat. In the Visitor's Center is a bookstore, artifacts on exhibit, and a 30-minute film on the life of Frederick Douglass. A guided tour of his home, exactly as he left it when he died, lasts about 20 minutes. Open daily 9 AM–5 PM; during winter months, 9 AM–4 PM. The Tourmobile stops here June 15 through Labor Day. See also TOURS.

**Octagon House** 1799 New York Avenue, N.W. (downtown); 638-3105. Presidential residence in 1814. Historic architectural exhibits. On the grounds of the American Institute of Architects. Tuesday–Friday, 10–4; weekends, 1–4.

**Old Stone House** 3051 M Street, N.W. (Georgetown); 426-6851. Built in 1765, one of the oldest structures in Washington, in what was once a busy commercial center and slave quarter. Open daily, 9:30–5; closed Monday–Tuesday, January through March.

**Petersen House** 516 10th Street, N.W. (downtown); 426-6830. Across from Ford's Theatre, this is the place where Abraham Lincoln died. Daily, 9–5; closed Christmas Day.

**Sewall-Belmont House** 144 Constitution Avenue, N.E. (Capitol Hill); 546-1210. Headquarters of the National Woman's Party; exhibit of suffrage and equal rights memorabilia. Fine example of 18th-century Capitol Hill residence.

**Smithsonian Institution Building** 1000 Jefferson Drive, S.W. (on the Mall). designed by James Renwick and built in 1855, it was the first Smithsonian building (popularly known as the "Castle"). For information on other parts of Smithsonian, see MUSEUMS.

**Woodrow Wilson House** 2340 S Street, N.W.; 387-4062. President Wilson's home from 1921–1924. Tuesday–Friday, 10–2; weekends, noon–4. Closed all of January and weekdays during February. Adults, $2.50; senior citizens and students up to 18 years, $1. National Trust members, free.

**Sights**

# Other Sights

**Hillwood Museum** 4155 Linnean Avenue, N.W.; 686-0410. Tour reservations, 686-5807. Museum Gift Shop, 686-1144. Hillwood is the home of the late Marjorie Merriweather Post. Her home, displaying the noted collection of Russian decorative art (including pieces by Fabergé) and French decorative art, is on view by reservation only. Also worth seeing are the surrounding grounds and buildings including an Adirondack-style lodge containing American Indian artifacts, a Russian dacha, greenhouse, gift shop, and the C.W. Post Wing exhibiting furnishings assembled around the turn of the century by Mrs. Post's father. Admission to the home and grounds. Note: children must be 12 years or older. Closed Sunday and Tuesday.

**Islamic Center** 2551 Massachusetts Avenue, N.W.; 332-8343. In the United States, this is the leading mosque. Daily, 10–5.

**John F. Kennedy Center for the Performing Arts** 2700 F Street, N.W. (Foggy Bottom); 254-3600. Tours daily at 10 and 1:15, lasting 40 minutes.

**National Aquarium** Basement of the Department of Commerce, 14th Street and Constitution Avenue, N.W., Room B-037; 377-2825. The nation's oldest aquarium (1873). Viewing time about 45 minutes. Admission fee.

**National Shrine of the Immaculate Conception** 4th Street and Michigan Avenue, N.E.; 526-8300. Largest Roman Catholic Church in the Western Hemisphere. Cafeteria, gift shop. Guided tours. Daily 7–6; open until 7 PM from April–October.

**Organization of American States, House of the Americas** 17th Street and Constitution Avenue, N.W., 20006; tour reservations, 789-3751. Formerly known as the Pan American Union. The 45-minute tour of this unusual building includes the Major Council Chamber, art gallery, Tropical Patio, Hall of Heroes and Flags, Francisco de Miranda Room, and the Aztec Gardens. Tours begin at 9:30 AM; the last tour is at 4 PM. Closed weekends and major holidays. See also Museum of Modern Art of Latin America under MUSEUMS—ART MUSEUMS.

**St. John's Church** 1525 H Street, N.W. (downtown at Lafayette Park); 347-8766. Classical design by Benjamin Latrobe. Many presidents have worshipped here. Daily 8 AM–4 PM.

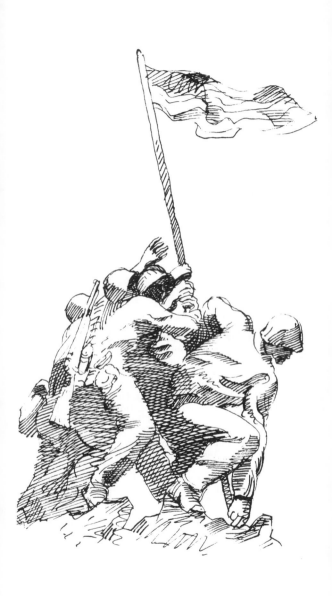

IWO JIMA MONUMENT

**Voice of America** 330 Independence Avenue, S.W., between 3rd and 4th Streets; 485-6231. News of America is broadcast 24 hours a day in English and 38 languages all over the world. Guided half-hour tours Monday–Friday at 8:45, 9:45, 10:45, 1:45, and 2:45.

**Washington National Cathedral** Wisconsin Avenue at Massachusetts Avenue and Woodley Street, N.W.; 537-6200. One of the last great Gothic cathedrals to be built. Sculpture of Abraham Lincoln kneeling in prayer, Helen Keller and Annie Sullivan Massey in crypt; President Wilson's tomb; space window containing a piece of moon rock. Open Monday–Saturday, 10–4:30; tours at 10 through 3:15; Sunday tours at 12:30 and 2 PM. Organ recitals frequently on Sunday at 5 PM. Organ demonstrations on Wednesdays at 12:15 PM. Pilgrim Observation Gallery open weekends during winter, Saturday, 10 AM to 3:45 PM and Sundays, 12:30 to 3:45 PM, with last tickets sold at 3:15. Admission charged to the Observation Gallery only. From this gallery you can see a fine view of the exterior of the Cathedral and of Washington from one of the highest points in the city. Cathedral aides wearing purple are eager to answer your questions. Expanded hours during warm season. For information on services, see RELIGIOUS SERVICES; see also MUSIC. Cathedral Herb Shop, gift shop, bookstore, and greenhouse.

**Washington Post Newspaper** 1150 15th Street, N.W., 20071; 334-6000. For tour reservations, 334-7969. Founded in 1877, this is one of the nation's leading newspapers. Tour includes the newsroom, composing room, printing presses, and explanation of paper's history. A working hot-type museum is part of the tour. Hourly tours by appointment are given Monday–Friday, 10–3. Children must be at least 12 years old.

See also TOURS; THINGS TO DO; PARKS AND NATURE PRESERVES.

# SKATING

## Ice Skating—All Outdoors

**Liberty Plaza Ice Rink** 1700 G Street, N.W. (downtown); 377-6598. Open late November, daily 11–8.

Skate rentals; group lessons; available for private rentals and parties. Lunchtime special rates between 11–1, Monday–Friday.

**Pershing Park** Pennsylvania Avenue between 14th and 15th Streets, N.W. (downtown).

**Sculpture Garden Outdoor Ice-Skating Rink** Between 7th and 9th Streets, N.W., across from National Archives and National Gallery of Art; 347-9041 (recorded announcement giving hours, fees and skate rental information). Public sessions daily during the winter; skate rentals and sharpening; 160' by 103' ice surface.

## Roller Skating

**Rock Creek Park** Beach Drive between Broad Branch Road and Ross Drive is closed to cars and open to skaters and bicyclers from 7 AM Saturday to 7 PM Sunday unless the following Monday is a holiday, in which case the Drive is closed through 7 PM Monday. For information, 426-7717.

# SPECIALTY AND GIFT SHOPS

Here is a sampling of unusual shops in Washington.

**Artifactory** 641 Indiana Avenue, N.W. (downtown); 393-2727. African art, imported clothes, and jewelry from exotic places for men, women, and children.

**As Time Goes By** 655 C Street, S.E., alongside Eastern Market; 543-7877. First-rate quality vintage clothing, accessories, and jewelry from the Victorian period through the fifties, for men and women.

**Batik Walla** 1615 Connecticut Avenue, N.W.; 462-6460. Afghanistanian, Pakistani, Indian, and other Asian handcrafts and clothing for women.

**Blue Moon** 2435 18th Street, N.W. (Adams Morgan); 265-8113. Retrospective and progressive styles in clothing for men and women, furniture, gift and novelty items, postcards and greeting cards.

**Chocolate Moose** 1800 M Street, N.W. (near Farragut North Metro stop); 463-0992. Not big on candy but rather a unique gift shop with a special selection of antique costume and handcrafted jewelry.

**Classic Clothing Co., Inc.** 1015 Wisconsin Avenue, N.W. (Georgetown); 965-2120. Vintage clothing boutique for men and women.

**Commander Salamander** 1420 Wisconsin Avenue, N.W. (Georgetown); 337-2265 or 333-9599. Very punk and all kinds of way-out fashions for men, women, and children, including T-shirts, jewelry, and cards.

**Geraldine's Rental Gowns** 4105 Wisconsin Avenue, N.W. (uptown); 686-5050. Costumes for men and women; tuxedos and tails; specializing in dresses and gowns for any occasion.

**Hats in the Belfry** 1237 Wisconsin Avenue, N.W. (Georgetown between M and N Streets); 342-2006. An incredible hat shop for men and women.

**Jameson & Hawkins** 2910 M Street, N.W. (Georgetown); 965-6911. A collection of select vintage Victorian dresses and antique jewelry. Also one-of-a-kind formal evening wear made by Washington designers.

**Liberty** 1513 Wisconsin Avenue, N.W. (Georgetown); 337-5742. Nice fabrics and unusual French and British fashion for men and women.

**Smull's Gallery/Gifts** 2031 Florida Avenue, N.W. (Dupont Circle Metro stop, Q Street exit); 232-8282. Clothes with character for women; gifts; jewelry.

**Splash** 1419 22nd Street, N.W.; 296-8325. Trendy gifts and cards similar to shops characteristic of Greenwich Village and San Francisco. Specialty T-shirts.

**Toast & Strawberries** 2009 R Street, N.W. (Dupont Circle); 234-2424. Also at Connecticut Avenue and R Street, N.W.; 234-1212. Handmade clothes and accessories from Africa and the Third World.

**United Nations Association Gift Shop** 3143 N Street, N.W. (Georgetown); 337-5553. Clothing and crafts from around the world; UNICEF cards and games.

The Washington National Cathedral, the Library of Congress, the National Trust for Historic Preservation (1600 H Street, N.W.; 673-4197), the Textile Museum, and all the museums of the Smithsonian have unique shops where you will find, among other things, the best souvenirs Washington has to offer.

# SPORTING ACTIVITIES AND EVENTS

For up-to-date information on all varieties of sports such as fishing, caving, cycling, hiking, field hockey, rafting, skating, skiing—you name it—consult the "Sporting Life" column of the "Weekend" section of Friday's *Washington Post*. Also consult the March issue of the *Washingtonian*, which by way of introducing the newcomer to the city includes information on sporting activities and events.

## Ticket Information

**Baseball, Baltimore Orioles:** 301/243-9800. (See **Memorial Stadium** under STADIUMS AND SPORTS ARENAS.)
**Basketball, Bullets:** 350-2100. (See **Capital Centre** under STADIUMS AND SPORTS ARENAS.)
**Football, Redskins:** 546-2222. (See **StarPlex-RFK Stadium** under STADIUMS AND SPORTS ARENAS.)
**Ice Hockey, Capitals:** 350-2100. (See **Capital Centre**.)
*Note*: If tickets are sold out, consult the classified ads of the *Washington Post* for ticketholders who wish to sell their tickets for a particular game.

# SPORTING GOODS

**Abercrombie & Fitch** In Georgetown Park at 3222 M Street, N.W.; 965-6500. Fine men's and women's sporting apparel, gifts, and the best in selected sporting equipment. Branch in Virginia.
**Eddie Bauer, Inc.** 1800 M Street, N.W.; 331-8009. This well-known sporting-goods business specializes in a broad selection of high-quality equipment and apparel for camping, hiking, boating, and sightseeing.
**Hudson Trail Outfitters, Ltd.** 4437 Wisconsin Avenue, N.W. (at Tenley Circle, uptown); 363-9810. also in The Shops at National Place, 13th and F Streets, N.W.; 393-1244. Wilderness outfitting specialists.

**Moss Brown & Co., Inc.** The Running Store 1522 Wisconsin Avenue, N.W. at P Street; 965-4350. Running clothes, shoes, and gear. Watch for new addresses.

See also BICYCLES AND BICYCLING.

# STADIUMS AND SPORTS ARENAS

**Capital Centre** 1 Harry S. Truman Drive, Landover, MD. 20785; 350-3900 for events and ticket information or 350-3400 for general information. The Washington Bullets basketball team and the Washington Capitals hockey team play here. Tickets to any event held at the Capital Centre may be purchased from the Hecht Company department stores or from the Capital Centre Downtown Ticket Office, 19th and L Streets, N.W., in the W. Bell Company, Monday–Friday, 10–6, or at the Capital Centre Crystal City Ticket Office in the Crystal City Underground next to Emilio's Restaurant, Monday–Friday, 10–5.

From the Capital Beltway, Route 495, take Exit 15A or 17A and follow the signs. From downtown Washington allow 1 hour in rush-hour traffic; at other times allow 30 minutes. Not accessible by public transportation.

**Memorial Stadium** Home of the Baltimore Orioles, Baltimore, Md. 21218; 301/243-9800 for ticket information or 301/432-0200 to charge tickets by phone. To purchase tickets in Washington in person, stop by the Baseball Store and Ticket Outlet, 914 17th Street, N.W.; 347-2525. Open Monday–Friday, 9 AM–6 PM; Saturday, 10 AM–2 PM. Directions from Washington to Memorial Stadium: Take I-95 north to Baltimore and watch for signs for the Memorial Stadium (1000 block of East 33rd Street).

**StarPlex** D.C. Armory, 2001 East Capitol Street, S.E., and RFK Stadium, 22nd and East Capitol Streets, S.E.; 547-9077 for event and ticket information. The enclosed armory has events ranging from the International Horse Show in October to antique shows, home shows, flower shows, boxing and tennis matches, and the Ringling Bros. Barnum & Bailey Circus in late March. Events are well advertised. At the stadium you'll find the Washington Redskins football team. Stadium-Armory Metro stop.

# SUBWAY

See TRANSPORTATION—PUBLIC TRANSPORTATION.

# TAXIS

See TRANSPORTATION.

# TEA

See COFFEE AND TEA; AFTERNOON TEA.

# TELEPHONES

For information on Washington area codes, see INFORMATION.

# THEATERS

Recently described as the second largest theater city outside New York, Washington is blessed with a variety of theatrical productions at any time: plays for children (see CHILDREN AND CHILDREN'S THINGS—ENTERTAINMENT); plays by new playwrights; plays on their way to Broadway and those on their return from Broadway as well as a selection of classic theater. Shows are especially well advertised in the *Washington Post* "Weekend" section on Friday and in the "Show" section on Sunday. Also consult the Washington *Calendar of Events* (see INFORMATION).

Some theaters (Arena, Kreeger, National, Kennedy, and Smithsonian) offer special services for hearing- and sight-impaired individuals (see HANDICAPPED INDIVIDUALS' RESOURCES).

Tours are offered at The National, Ford's Theatre, and the Kennedy Center.

**District Curators** has program information on current avant-garde theater, performance arts, dance, and music around town; 783-0360.

**TicketPlace** 12th and F Streets on the Plaza; 842-5387 (TIC-KETS). Monday, noon–2; Tuesday–Saturday, 11–6 PM; closed Sunday. Cash only. Washington's only place to buy tickets half price on the day of the performance or full price in advance. Tickets sold for events at major theaters and stadiums. Hear recorded information by telephone.

Here is a fairly complete list of Washington's theaters and their box office telephone numbers.

**American National Theater** Kennedy Center; 254-3670. American and international productions.

**Arena Stage** 6th and M Streets, S.W. (waterfront area); 488-3300. Arena is the first theater outside New York to win a Tony Award for "theatrical excellence." (See also **Kreeger Theater**; under NIGHTLIFE—SOUTHWEST, see **Old Vat Room**.)

**The Barns of the Wolf Trap Foundation** 1635 Trap Road, Vienna, Va. 22180; 703/938-2404. This small theater, seating 364, was formerly a barn built in the early 1700s by Johann Peter Kniskern in upstate New York. Take Route 7 (Leesburg Pike) west of Tysons Corner, Virginia, to the Wolf Trap sign and turn left. Go through the park and past the Filene Center, continuing on Trap Road to the sign for "The Barns." Productions, including concerts, movies, mime, and children's theater, are held during the fall, winter, and spring. Three weeks of opera during the summer.

**d.c. space** 443 7th Street, N.W. at E Street (downtown); 347-4960. Various theater companies perform here; watch their advertisements for box office telephone numbers. Gallery Place Metro stop.

**Filene Center II at Wolf Trap** 1624 Trap Road, Vienna, Va. 22180; ticket information, 301/255-1860 or 800/223-1814. Performances all summer long in the open air. For directions, see listing under MUSIC.

**Ford's Theatre** 511 10th Street, N.W. (Metro Center Metro stop, 11th Street exit); 347-4833. The renovated theater hosts popular plays year-round. Also see SIGHTS WORTH SEEING—LANDMARKS AND HISTORIC HOMES.

**Horizons Theatre** Grace Episcopal Church, 1041 Wisconsin Avenue, N.W.; 342-7706.

**John F. Kennedy Center for the Performing Arts** 2700 F Street, N.W. (Foggy Bottom). Concert Hall, 254-3776; Opera House, 254-3770; Eisenhower Theater, 254-3670; Terrace Theater, 254-9895; American National Theater, 457-8345; American Film Institute Theater, 785-4600; general information, 254-3600; Hearing Impaired, TTY 254-3906. Instant Charge, 857-0900; group sales of 20 or more, 634-7201. For tour information, call 254-3774.

**Kreeger Theater at Arena Stage** 6th Street and Maine Avenue, S.W. (waterfront area); 488-3300.

**The National** 1321 Pennsylvania Avenue, N.W.; ticket information, 628-6161. Oldest continually operating theater in the country. Free events include Saturday Morning at the National (for children) and Monday Night at the National (for adults); call 783-3372 for recorded message and to make a reservation. For further information and reservations for free tour, call 783-3370. Metro Center or Federal Triangle Metro stop.

**New Playwrights' Theatre** 1742 Church Street, N.W. (Dupont Circle); 232-1122. New Playwrights' holds readings of new plays and productions of plays in stages of revision as well as full productions. Dupont Circle Metro stop.

**Scene Shop At Arena Stage** 6th and M Streets, S.W.; 488-3300. A simple stage and 150 seats compose this theater which allows for the exploration of "uneasy" plays.

**The Shakespeare Theatre at the Folger** 201 East Capitol Street, S.E.; 546-4000. Warm, intimate theater where Shakespeare's and others' plays are produced.

**Smithsonian Performing Arts** 357-1500. Events are held at the following locations: Baird Auditorium: Museum of Natural History, 10th Street and Constitution Avenue, N.W.; Discovery Theater: Arts & Industries Building, 900 Jefferson Drive, S.W.; Hall of Musical Instruments: Museum of American History, 14th Street and Constitution Avenue, N.W.; Hirshhorn Auditorium: Hirshhorn Museum and Sculpture Garden, 7th Street and Independence Avenue, S.W.; Renwick Grand Salon: Renwick Gallery, 17th Street and Pennsylvania Avenue, N.W.

**Source Theatre** 1809 14th Street, N.W. (at S Street); 462-1073. Home of the Source Theatre Company, which also performs at other locations in Washington.

**Studio Theatre** 1401 Church Street, N.W. 265-7412. Productions September through June. Tickets also available at TicketPlace.

**Trapier Theater at St. Alban's** Wisconsin and Massachusetts Avenues, N.W., adjacent to the Washington National Cathedral; 537-6537.

**Warehouse Rep** 1835 14th Street, N.W.; 462-1073.

**Warner Theater** 513 13th Street, N.W. (downtown); 626-1050. Metro Center or Federal Triangle Metro stop.

**Woolly Mammoth Theatre Co.** 1317 G Street, N.W. (Church of the Epiphany); 393-3939. Metro Center Metro stop. Features a season of intriguing contemporary comedy and drama, performed by an acclaimed resident acting troupe.

# THINGS TO DO

**Discover brass rubbing** a traditional English craft, at the London Brass Rubbing Centre in Washington at the Washington National Cathedral Gift Shop Crypt, Mount Saint Alban, Washington, D.C. 20016; 244-9328. Over 60 facsimile brasses to choose from, ranging in price from $1.75 through $17 for a full life-size height. No age limit; family groups welcome. Monday–Saturday, 9–5; Sunday, 9:30–5:30.

**Listen to the bells** at the Washington National Cathedral ring after the 11 AM service every Sunday (usually lasting 15 minutes) and on major holidays. Sometimes a full peal is successful and lasts 3½ hours. On New Year's Day the peal is at noon.

**Enjoy the peaceful view** of Washington from Arlington Cemetery. At the John F. Kennedy Memorial or from the Tomb of the Unknown Soldier the view is magnificent. The Bishop's Garden at the Washington National Cathedral is also serene (when children aren't playing hide-and-seek among the boxwood!).

**Visit the outdoor fish market** on Maine Avenue, S.W.,

on the waterfront. Here you can buy fresh eels, oysters, and the famous Chesapeake Bay live crabs.

**Go horseback riding** in Rock Creek Park. Rock Creek Horse Center, Military and Glover Roads, N.W.; 362-0117. Fee charged.

**Visit the Old Post Office Observation Tower** located in the Old Post Office Building (The Pavilion) at Pennsylvania Avenue and 12th Street, N.W. The tour of the bell tower is given 9 AM–5 PM daily, 8 AM–11 PM April through September. The bell ringers rehearse Thursday evening, 7–9:30 PM; 523-5691. The view from the tower is absolutely magnificent—just high enough for a perspective angle, but close enough for the detail.

**Ride the mule-drawn barge** on the C&O Canal, departing from the landing at 30th and Thomas Jefferson Streets, N.W. Departure times mid-morning through late afternoon Wednesdays–Sundays. Tickets may be purchased 2 hours in advance of departure from the Foundry Mall Visitor Center, 1055 Thomas Jefferson Place, N.W.; 472-4376. Operates from mid-April through mid-October. Operated by the National Park Service. Fee charged.

**Attend a session of the Supreme Court** (See SIGHTS WORTH SEEING—GOVERNMENT IN ACTION.)

**Attend an open hearing** of a Senate or House Committee. See the *Washington Post* for schedules published daily.

**Watch an art demonstration** at the Art Barn on Sundays from 1–3 PM (2401 Tilden Street, N.W.; 426-6719).

**Monday Night at the National** focuses on informal and sometimes experimental theater and musical evenings in the Helen Hayes Gallery, 1321 Pennsylvania Avenue, N.W. (Metro Center Metro stop, 13th Street exit); 783-3372. Free.

**Take in the Marine Corps Sunset Parade** one of the best shows in town—and it's free! Friday evenings at 8:15, May through early September, at the Marine Barracks, 8th and I Streets, S.E. Two-hour performance of music and precision marching featuring Marine Band, Drum and Bugle Corps, and the Silent Drill Platoon. Reservations required 3 weeks in advance. Call 433-6060 or write to Adjutant, U.S. Marine Corps, Marine Barracks, 8th and I Streets, S.E., Washington,

D.C. 20390. Directions and parking information will be mailed. A one-hour Sunset Parade is held Tuesday evenings, May–August, at 7 PM, at the Iwo Jima Memorial, Arlington, Virginia. No reservations needed. Sit on a blanket or bring your own chairs and enjoy the view of Washington as well! Call 433-6060 for parking information and directions.

# TIPPING

It is not the habit of this city to include a charge for service as part of the bill. Therefore you should know that people here are usually satisfied with a 15 percent tip, whether you are thanking a taxicab driver or a waiter at your favorite restaurant (remember to figure the tip on the total before sales tax).

Tip porters a minimum of $1, and 50¢ per bag for more than 2 bags (unless one weighs a ton, in which case you might want to be generous). It is not necessary to tip doormen or parking-lot attendants, but many people do so. If you are a guest at a hotel and uncertain of the policy, ask the manager for guidance. At the theater do not tip the usher; the general programs are free.

# TOBACCO

**A. Garfinkle, Inc.** 1585 I Street, N.W.; 638-1175.
**Georgetown Tobacco & Pipe Store, Inc.** 3144 M Street, N.W.; 338-5100.
**Metropolitan Cigar & Tobacco** 921 19th Street, N.W.; 223-9648.
**National Pipe & Tobacco Shop** 1747 Pennsylvania Avenue, N.W.; 466-2338.
**Tinder Box** 5310 Wisconsin Avenue, N.W., in Mazza Gallerie; 686-5445.
**W. Curtis Draper Tobacconist, Inc.** 507 11th Street, N.W. (downtown); 638-2555. Also at 1122 Connecticut Avenue, N.W.; 785-2226.

# TOURS

Listed here are only a few of the agencies offering tours to Washington. Tours are also given of the art museums and the historical, scientific, and military museums, and of the sights worth seeing. When making inquiries, ask about the frequency and length of the tour.

**Tourmobile** 554-7950 (recorded message). Sightseeing around the Mall and Arlington Cemetery couldn't be easier. Tours also to Mount Vernon during the Cherry Blossom Festival and through Thanksgiving, subject to demand and weather. Tours also to the Frederick Douglass Home, June 15–Labor Day. Hours vary depending on the season but are generally 9 AM to 5 PM or later. Set your own pace because you may reboard a Tourmobile any time you want. Tourguides are on board and the Tourmobiles are accessible to handicapped individuals. For a van with a wheelchair lift, make your reservation 24 hours in advance by calling 554-7020. The 554-7950 telephone number is a 24-hour recorded message that tells you the stops on each tour and how to buy your ticket.

Tickets may be purchased at the Tourmobile booths at the Washington Monument, Lincoln Memorial, Arlington National Cemetery, or at any of the stops. For information not on the recorded message, call 554-7020. Tickets purchased after 2 PM are good for that day and, for a small extra charge, good for the next day as well. Tourmobile has been in operation since 1969 and has seved more than 19 million visitors.

**D.C. Tour Guide Service** 839-3498. Provides guides for tour buses; for smaller groups the service will provide a van. Guides are available in any language requested.

**Gray Line Sightseeing Tours** 4th and E Streets, S.W., Washington, D.C. 20024; 479-5900. All-day deluxe tour of Washington, Arlington National Cemetery, Alexandria, and Mount Vernon (Tour A). Other tours include interiors of public buildings, Embassy Row, and Washington after Dark. (Gray Line is an international sightseeing organization. If your travel agent does not have a brochure on Washington, request one at the above address.)

**Old Town Trolley** 639-4037. This colorful trolley takes a pleasant 2-hour ride from Capitol Hill at the Hyatt Regency Hotel down Pennsylvania Avenue, stopping at Ford's Theatre, The Shops at National Place, and the J. W. Marriott Hotel. Then it goes on its way to the White House, Stephen Decatur House, Capitol Hilton Hotel, up Connecticut Avenue, stopping at the Mayflower, Washington Hilton, and Sheraton Washington hotels, to the National Zoo. The trolley travels over to the Kalorama-Embassy Row neighborhood and museum district, stopping along the way at the Woodrow Wilson House (see MUSEUMS, **Dupont Kalorama Museum Consortium**). Then it winds its way into Georgetown by the Oak Hill Cemetery and Dumbarton Oaks Gardens and Museum, down Wisconsin Avenue, stopping at Georgetown Park (see SHOPPING MALLS AND CENTERS). The trolley heads toward the Lincoln Memorial, along the Mall, and back up to the Hyatt Regency on New Jersey Avenue. Begin your tour at any of 11 stops, disembarking for shopping, dining, or sightseeing along the way. Reboard when ready, using only one ticket. The trolley travels every 15 minutes in the summertime and every 30 minutes the remainder of the year. The recorded message will provide information on prices and hours of service.

**Washington Boat Lines, Inc.** Pier 4, 6th and Water Streets, S.W.; 554-8011. Sightseeing on the Potomac from late March through October. Take a photo cruise, a half-day cruise to Mount Vernon, a 1-hour cruise on the Potomac River around the monuments and Georgetown (also available in the evening, lasting 2 hours), or a moonlight or teen dance cruise (see NIGHTLIFE—SOUTHWEST). Docks also at Lincoln Memorial and Mount Vernon.

# Walking Tours and Garden Tours

House, garden, and embassy tours are popular in April and May in Washington. See ANNUAL EVENTS for further information.

**Smithsonian Associates** sponsors walking tours of Washington from time to time. For a schedule, call 357-2700.

**Walking tours on your own** are made very worthwhile by using one of these books: *A Walking Guide to His-*

*toric Georgetown; Washington on Foot; A Guide to the Architecture of Washington, D.C.* (For bibliographic information, see BOOKS, BOOKSHOPS, AND BOOK SALES—GUIDES TO WASHINGTON.)

A **Dupont Kalorama Museum Walk** brochure is available at the Tourist Information Center, Great Hall, U.S. Department of Commerce (see INFORMATION), or from places on the tour. The brochure is well designed and includes an easy-to-read-and-understand map of neighborhood galleries, hotels, and the following museums: the Phillips Collection, Textile Museum, Woodrow Wilson House, Anderson House, Columbia Historical Society, Barney Studio House, and Fondo Del Sol Visual Art and Media Center. (See MUSEUMS.)

# A Do-It-Yourself One-Day Tour of the City

As a first-time visitor to Washington, start your morning by visiting the Tourist Information Center in the Great Hall of the Department of Commerce (see INFORMATION). You can park your car across the street on 15th Street, and have breakfast in the Commerce Department's cafeteria.

From the Tourist Center, walk down to the Washington Monument, where you should take the free elevator ride to the top to view the city Pierre L'Enfant planned so well. (See SIGHTS WORTH SEEING—CEMETERIES AND MEMORIALS.)

From the Washington Monument, board the Tourmobile, which, for a fee, will take you to Washington's major attractions. You can get off wherever you wish and reboard when you wish. The Tourmobile Information Center is at the Washington Monument. (See TOURS.)

The best places to eat lunch on the Mall are at the National Gallery of Art, but lines are long. If you are a Smithsonian Associate, you may choose to have a great lunch in the Associates Cafe at the National Museum of Natural History, which also has a fast-food cafeteria. Other excellent places to dine along the Tourmobile route are the government cafeterias in the James Madison Building of the Library of Congress; the cafeterias in various House and Senate office buildings; or in the Supreme Court. There are also numerous restaurants on Capitol Hill. (See RESTAURANTS.)

Your day will probably be over by the time you finish your Tourmobile route.

*Note*: To avoid complete exhaustion and "museum fatigue," consider concentrating your visits to specific exhibits within one or two of the museums and galleries.

# Another Do-It-Yourself One-Day Tour of the City

For the visitor who wants to see something other than the museums and galleries around the Mall, consider the following:

Begin your day with a tour of the Washington National Cathedral. Be sure to go up to the Pilgrim Observation Gallery for a fine view of the city. (See SIGHTS WORTH SEEING—OTHER SIGHTS.)

For lunch try the Sushiko, a small Japanese restaurant, or Old Europe, a small German restaurant, both just south of the Cathedral on Wisconsin Avenue in the northern part of Georgetown.

Spend the afternoon touring Dumbarton Oaks Museum and Gardens, located off Wisconsin Avenue at R Street to the east (see MUSEUMS—ART MUSEUMS; PARKS AND NATURE PRESERVES). Or continue down Wisconsin Avenue to the heart of Georgetown, where you can take a self-guided walking tour. See the map of Georgetown in this book or use one of the references listed under BOOKS, BOOKSHOPS, AND BOOK SALES—GUIDES TO WASHINGTON.

An alternative to Dumbarton Oaks would be to see the Phillips Collection and/or Textile Museum (see MUSEUMS: ART MUSEUMS). They are off Massachusetts Avenue south of the Cathedral. On your way down Massachusetts you will pass the Naval Observatory, the Vice President's mansion, and what is familiarly known as "Embassy Row." Restaurant Nora is a nice place to have lunch (see RESTAURANTS). Request a copy of the *Dupont Kalorama Museum Walk* pamphlet from the Phillips Collection or Textile Museum. Woodrow Wilson House, Anderson House, Columbia Historical Society, and other museums and galleries are in this neighborhood.

# Pennsylvania Avenue Development Tour

Stretching from the U.S. Capitol to the White House, Pennsylvania Avenue is the "Nation's Main Street." For nearly two hundred years this ceremonial route has been used for presidential inaugural parades and funeral processions. This area long ago was a thriving commerical center where Matthew Brady had his photography studio (near 7th and Pennsylvania), and the Willard Hotel (at 14th Street) played host to important glitterati. However, over time the popular commercial areas moved westward toward Connecticut Avenue and Georgetown, and the heart of Pennsylvania Avenue declined.

In 1972 the U.S. Congress established the Pennsylvania Avenue Development Corporation to revitalize this historic area. Much of the renovation is finished and readily apparent: 15th Street at Pershing Park sports a splendid ice-skating rink in the winter and a café year-round. The Willard Hotel is once again a magnificent host, as is its neighbor, the Hotel Washington. At 14th Street, Western Plaza displays a paving design based on Pierre L'Enfant's 1791 plan for the Capital City. Notes on his original plan and quotations about the life of the nation's capital are carved into the granite surface. Bordering this to the north is the restored National Theatre, which is nestled within National Place (see SHOPPING MALLS AND CENTERS). At 11th Street is the fabulous restoration of the Old Post Office Building (see SHOPPING MALLS AND CENTERS), with its 315-foot bell tower and handsome atrium. And on toward the Capitol, between 10th and 9th Streets is the J. Edgar Hoover FBI Building, displaying 10 commemorative flags that surround the current 50-star U.S. flag and show the development of the Stars and Stripes since 1775.

This area has fine examples of vastly differing styles of architecture, from the 19th-century neoclassicism of the U.S. Capitol to the romanesque Revival style of the Old Post Office Building, to I. M. Pei's contemporary East Building of the National Gallery of Art. Along the south side of Pennsylvania Avenue between 6th Street (Federal Trade Commission) and 15th Street (Commerce Department) is the Federal

Triangle, a collection of grandiose Classical government buildings built in the late 1920s and 1930s, one of the most massive assemblages of this style extant today.

For further information and a map to this area, request "A Walker's Guide to Pennsylvania Avenue" (published by the Pennsylvania Avenue Development Corporation), available from the Washington Convention and Visitors Association's Tourist Information Center located at the west end of the development plan (see INFORMATION). For information on the architectural history of this area, read *A Guide to the Architecture of Washington, D.C.* (see BOOKS, BOOKSHOPS, AND BOOK SALES—GUIDES TO WASHINGTON), which is organized into tours you can take by car or foot.

# TOYS

**Chevy Chase Novelty Shop, Inc.** 3807 McKinley Street, N.W. (just off Connecticut near Chevy Chase Circle at the Maryland line); 966-7011.

**F.A.O. Schwarz** At Mazza Gallerie, 5300 Wisconsin Avenue, N.W.; 363-8455. Also at Georgetown Park, 3222 M Street, N.W.; 342-2285.

**Little Toy Park** 3251 Prospect Street, N.W. (Georgetown); 342-0050. Sophisticated puzzles and assorted intriguing toys.

**Red Balloon** 1073 Wisconsin Avenue, N.W. (Georgetown); 965-1200. Imported and domestic clothing and toys.

**Sullivan's Toys, Inc.** 3412 Wisconsin Avenue, N.W. (uptown); 362-1343. Dolls, models, books, art supplies, stuffed animals, etc.

**Tree Top Toys, Inc.** 3301 New Mexico Avenue, N.W., at Foxhall Square (near American University); 244-3500. Toys for children, including stuffed animals, records and tapes; also Aprica strollers.

See also CHILDREN AND CHILDREN'S THINGS—CLOTHES AND TOY SHOPS.

# TRANSPORTATION

## Public Transportation

Public transportation in the Washington area is served by the Washington Metropolitan Area Transit Authority. There are 2 systems: **Metrobus** and **Metrorail** (subway). Large maps of the bus routes are sold in drugstores and grocery stores and at the Metro offices, 600 5th Street, N.W., Washington, D.C. 20001. Lobby hours are Monday–Friday, 8:30 AM–4 PM.

Metrorail station attendants have Metrobus schedules and Metrorail information. *All About Metro* is a free brochure which includes a map, parking information, transfer procedures, location of bicycle locker rentals, and rush-hour fares.

For both systems, the following numbers are helpful:

Scheduling and routing information (6 AM–11:30 PM): 637-7000. (TDD: 638-3780).

Timetables by mail (Monday–Friday, 8–4:30): 637-1261.

Lost & found (Monday–Friday, 8:30–4:30): 962-1195.

Transit police (24 hours daily): Emergency, 962-1289, or 962-2121.

Metrobus consumer assistance (Monday–Friday, 8:30–4): 637-1328.

Metro has a reduced-fare program for senior citizens and handicapped individuals. Identification cards are required. Additional information for senior citizens: 637-7000. Additional information for handicapped individuals: 962-1245 or 1246.

**Hours of Operation** *Metrobus* operates 24 hours daily on some routes, with reduced frequency at night, on weekends, and on holidays.

*Metrorail* operates Monday–Friday, 6 AM to midnight; Saturday, 8 AM to midnight; Sunday, 10 AM–midnight. Rush hours on Metrobus and Metrorail are 6 AM–9:30 AM and 3 PM–6:30 PM.

**Fares** *Metrobus* fares must be exact change—the driver cannot make change. Tokens and transfers may be used. At this writing the base fare on Metrobus traveling anywhere in Washington is 75¢.

*Metrorail* fares are paid by farecard, which must be purchased before boarding the train. Detailed instructions and personnel help you in this procedure. Base fare is 80¢.

Fares on Metrobus and Metrorail are higher during rush hours. There is a reduced-fare program for senior citizens and handicapped individuals—telephone information above. Children 5 and under ride free—2 children per paying passenger.

Family Tour Fares are available for specific days of the weekend (637-7000).

**Bicycles** Bicycle locker rentals are available at many stations: 962-1327. To take your bicycle on Metrorail, you'll need a permit ($15 for 5 years). You may take your bike on rail weekdays after 7 PM, Saturdays, Sundays, and holidays except for the 4th of July. Call 962-1116 for further information or pick up brochure *All About Metro* at a Metrorail station.

# Taxis

Taxis are plentiful in Washington, especially at the airports. However, if you need to call one, here are a few numbers to try (all serving you 24 hours daily):
Capitol Cab: 546-2400.
Diamond Cab: 387-6200.
Yellow Cab: 544-1212.

It is not a bad idea to get into the habit of jotting down the cab company, car number, and driver's name so that if you leave anything in the taxi or need to file a complaint (or compliment), you will have the appropriate information. Here are some useful telephone numbers:
For *compliments*, call the cab company.
For *complaints on interstate service*, call 331-1671.
For *complaints on service within Washington*, call 727-5401.

For **lost and found**, the police precinct nearest the place you alighted may have the item. If you know the name, number, and fleet of your taxi driver, call 727-5401.

# Taxi Fares

Fares in Washington are based on zones, with surcharges for traveling during the rush hour. The driver is able to give you an accurate estimate of the fare to your destination. Fares to the airports are based on mileage.

*Note*: See information listed below under AIRPORTS for approximate taxi fares to the center of Washington. It is not unusual to get ripped off by a driver, especially if he thinks you are from out of town, and be charged $50 when the fare should be $7 maximum! Always get a receipt, and always *verify the information* on the receipt as to cab number, driver's name, cab company, and license plate number if you can. If you feel you have been overcharged, call the Washington Metropolitan Area Transit Commission, 1625 I Street, N.W., Room 316, Washington, D.C. 20006; 331-1671. However, if you do not have at least a receipt with the taxi number and name of the taxi company and date and time of your trip, there is little WMATC can do for you. The office is open Monday–Friday, 8–4:30 PM.

## Car and Limousine Rental

Rental prices vary within the same company, with higher rental rates at the places of greatest demand, such as the airports. Of the many car rental businesses in Washington, here are a few:

**Avis** 800/331-1212. Locations: Washington National Airport, 379-4757; Dulles International Airport, 471-5975; 1722 M Street, N.W., 467-6585; and Union Station (Amtrak), 50 Massachusetts Avenue, N.W., 789-0742.

**Budget Rent-a-Car** In the Washington area: 628-2750; outside the Washington area: 800/527-0700. Locations: Washington National Airport, 703/739-0000; Dulles International Airport, 301/437-9373; 12th and K Streets, N.W., 628-2750.

**Hertz** 800/654-3131. Locations: Washington National Airport; Dulles International Airport; 1622 L Street, N.W., 659-8702; and Union Station (Amtrak), 50 Massachusetts Avenue, N.W., 789-0460. Also at New York Avenue and 11th Street, N.W., 628-6174.

Of the many limousine services available in Washington, here is one:

**Carey Limousine Service** 892-2000. In nearby Virginia suburbs. Telephones on most cars; bilingual; 24-hour service; stretch limos and Rolls-Royces available; they'll tour you around town or anywhere in the United States.

# Airports Serving Washington

**Washington National Airport** is the closest to the city. Transportation into Washington by *taxi* (fare based on mileage) costs about $7. Distance into the city is approximately 5–7 miles. If there is more than one passenger, each additional passenger is $1. The base fare is charged only once. Let the driver know you are traveling as a group. See information under TAXIS. Transportation into Washington by *airport limousine* costs approximately $5, or by *Metrorail* (Washington's subway system), National Airport Metro stop, about $1.60.

**Dulles International Airport** (designed by Eero Saarinen) is in Chantilly, Virginia, about 25 miles west of Washington. Transportation into the city is by *taxi*, approximately $30, and $1 for each additional passenger. One person should pay the fare and let the driver know you are traveling as a group; otherwise the driver is likely to charge the base rate to each passenger. See information under TAXIS. By *airport limousine*, approximately $10.

**Baltimore-Washington International Airport** (BWI) is about 36 miles northeast of Washington or about 45 minutes. Transportation is by *taxi*, approximately $35; by *airport limousine*, approximately $10; or by *Amtrak train service* from the BWI station to Union Station, approximately $8.75. A shuttle bus runs between the airport and the BWI station.

# Airport Limousine Services

**ABC Baggage Carriers** BWI limousine service. Serves Baltimore-Washington International Airport and Washington National Airport from BWI; 441-2345. Pick up at the Capitol Hilton, 16th and K Streets, N.W., and the Washington Hilton, Connecticut Avenue and T Street, N.W. See AIRPORTS SERVING WASHINGTON (above) for information on fares.

**Washington Flyer** Serves Washington National and Dulles International Airports; 685-1400. Pick up at the following hotels: Washington Hilton, 1919 Connecticut Avenue, N.W., and Capitol Hilton, 16th and K Streets, N.W. See AIRPORTS SERVING WASHINGTON (above) for information on fares.

## Bus Terminals Serving Washington

**Greyhound Terminal** 1110 New York Avenue, N.W. between 11th and 12th Streets; 565-2662.
**Trailways Terminal** 1st and L Street, N.E.; 737-5800.

## Train Station Serving Washington

The intercity rail transportation system in the United States is called **Amtrak**. Amtrak arrives in town at Union Station, 50 Massachusetts Avenue and North Capitol Street, N.W. Amtrak schedule information, 484-7540; Metroliner, 484-5580. Also, 800/USA-RAIL (872-7245). Amtrak headquarters, 383-3000.

# UNIVERSITIES AND LEARNING CENTERS

A few of the major universities in the Washington area are listed here. See the white pages of the telephone directory for direct-dial numbers to the various departments, libraries, and programs.

**American University** Massachusetts Avenue and Nebraska Avenue, N.W., 20016; 686-2000.

**Catholic University of America** 620 Michigan Avenue, N.E., 20064; 635-5000. Brookland-CUA Metro stop.

**First Class, Inc.** 1522 Connecticut Avenue, N.W., 20036; (Dupont Circle Metro stop, Q Street exit); 797-5102. The best professionals available are chosen to teach a variety of one-night or weekend seminars ranging in topics from art to travel with an emphasis on business and career development. Each seminar lasts 2 or 3 hours, and the average cost is $15. Request a list of classes by phone.

**Gallaudet College** 7th Street and Florida Avenue, N.E., 20002; 651-5000. Gallaudet College is the only college for the deaf in the world offering liberal arts. An associate degree for hearing interpreters is also offered.

**George Washington University** 2121 I Street, N.W., 20052 (Foggy Bottom); 676-6000. School of Medicine and Health Sciences, 2300 I Street, N.W.; 676-3506.

# GEORGETOWN

George Washington University Hospital, 901 23rd Street, N.W.; 676-3125. Lisner Auditorium, 21st and H Streets, N.W.; 676-6800. Charles E. Smith Athletic Center ticket office, 600 22nd Street, N.W.; 676-5900. Foggy Bottom Metro stop.

**Georgetown University** 37th and O Streets, N.W., 20064; 625-0100. Law Center, 600 New Jersey Avenue, N.W.; 624-8000. Medical School, 3900 Reservoir Road, N.W.; 625-4932. Dental School, 3900 Reservoir Road, N.W.; 625-4932. Georgetown University Hospital, 3800 Reservoir Road, N.W.: 625-0100.

**Howard University** 2400 5th Street, N.W. (at T Street), 20059; 636-6100. College of Medicine, 520 W Street, N.W.; 636-6270. Howard University Hospital, 2041 Georgia Avenue, N.W.; 745-6100.

**Johns Hopkins University School of Advanced International Studies** 1740 Massachusetts Avenue, N.W., 20036; 785-6200. Dupont Circle Metro Stop.

**Open University, A Learning Annex Program** 3333 Connecticut Avenue, N.W., 20008 (Cleveland Park Metro stop); 966-9606. The variety of classes range from "Limousine Scavenger-Hunt Race" to "How to Travel on Your Own." The short-term low-tuition classes are especially popular with singles in the 28–40 age range. Request a current list of classes by phone or pick up a copy at your local grocery store or drugstore.

**University of the District of Columbia** 4200 Connecticut Avenue, N.W., 20008; 282-7300. Van Ness-UDC Metro stop.

# WEATHER

Washington is remembered for its very humid summers; mild to crisp autumns with Indian summer extending sometimes into November; wet winters with snow sometimes crippling the area in January and February; and cool-to-warm springs when tulips and daffodils decorate every park.

In the summer wear loose-fitting clothing to take advantage of the cooling breezes. Buildings are air-conditioned so it is wise to have a light jacket or sweater handy.

Fall temperatures range from 80°F in September to as low as 38°F in November with an average for the period of 58°F. Mornings are very chilly but by mid-afternoon it can be quite warm. Dress in layers so that you can adjust to the broad temperature ranges.

During the winter, the normal low for December through March is 27°F (in January) and the normal high is 53°F (in March). Being next to the Potomac

River, Washington tends to be quite wet, cold, and windy. In addition to the jackets and sweaters, remember to wear your scarf, hat, gloves, and boots (and long underwear). Just when you think you can't stand the cold weather anymore, there will be a break in the temperature when it can soar to 55°F or higher!

Springtime in Washington is as nice as autumn. The low is 44°F in April to a high of 83°F in June. Again the mornings and evenings can be chilly, so it is advisable to dress in layers.

Washington attracts high school classes from all over the nation in the spring and of course when school is out the tourists are in all summer long. That makes the autumn and winter months ideal for touring Washington at a leisurely pace.

## Weather Forecasts

For Washington and vicinity: 936-1212.

Boating forecast for Chesapeake Bay and river stage data: 899-3210.

Extended outlook for Virginia, Maryland, and Delaware: 899-3240.

2-day forecasts for 10 major Eastern cities: 899-3244.

2-day forecasts for 10 major Western cities: 899-3249.

# WINES AND LIQUORS

District law allows restaurant patrons to bring their own wine to the restaurant and the restaurant charges a "corkage fee." Always inquire about this service when making reservations.

**Capitol Hill Spirits** 323 Pennsylvania Avenue, S.E.; 543-2900. This sports a pretty good carryout deli in back (not open Saturdays).

**Central Liquor Store, Inc.** 518 9th Street, N.W. (downtown); 737-2800. Extra-large selection of wine and liquor. Free parking across street with $15 minimum purchase.

**Eagle Wine & Cheese** 3345 M Street, N.W. (Georgetown); 333-5500. Liquor too.

**Pearson's Liquor & Wine Annex** 2436 Wisconsin Avenue, N.W. (Georgetown); 333-6666.

# WOMEN'S INTERESTS

**American Association of University Women** Headquarters, 2401 Virginia Avenue, N.W.; 785-7700. D.C. branch, 463-4273.

**D.C. Rape Crisis Center** 2201 P Street, N.W.; 333-7273 (hotline) or 232-0202. This resource, the first rape counseling center in the country, has a group for women who have experienced incest in their youth, as well as offering counseling for victims of sexual assault.

**George Washington University's Center for Continuing Education in Washington** (It offers programs for men also.) In the Academic Center, 801 22nd Street, N.W., Room T-409; 676-7036. Individual and group career counseling and certificate programs in such areas as information systems, paralegal profession, landscape design, publications, fund raising, administration, financial planning, and employee benefits.

**Georgetown Women's Club** 3251 Prospect Street, N.W.; 333-7650. By membership; guests accepted for a fee. The ultimate in-town retreat for women, offering services for hair, nails, skin, body care, and networking possibilities. Also, *private* whirlpools, habitat room, exercise room, and massage. Light fare served.

**League of Women Voters** National Office, 1730 M Street, N.W. (downtown); 429-1965.

**League of Women Voters of D.C.** 1341 G Street, N.W. (downtown); 347-3403.

**National Organization for Women** Headquarters, 1401 New York Avenue, N.W. (downtown); 347-2279.

**National Women's Education Fund** 624 9th Street, N.W.; 822-6636. Sponsors professional seminars around the country. Among local programs is the Washington Women's Network.

**Planned Parenthood of Metropolitan Washington**
1108 16th Street, N.W.; 347-8500. Educational programs, advocacy and clinical services. Clinic: 347-8512.

**Washington Women Outdoors** 2334 19th Street, N.W.; 797-8222. Offers a variety of outdoor activities including biking, hiking, rock climbing, camping, and workshops. Activities are listed in the "Sporting Life" column of "Weekend" in Friday's *Washington Post*.

**Women's National Bank** 1627 K Street, N.W. (downtown); 466-4090.

**YWCA** 624 9th Street, N.W.; 638-2100. Programs in health and fitness, education and training, the arts, and rehabilitation, and programs for children and youth.

# WOMEN'S WEAR

**Alcott & Andrews** 2000 Pennsylvania Avenue, N.W. (Farragut West Metro stop); 822-9476. Comprehensive collection of classic career and casual clothing.

**Britches for Women** 1200 18th Street, N.W.; 659-2444. Also in Georgetown Park; 337-6161. Very nice classic clothing and sportswear.

**Claire Dratch, Inc.** 1224 Connecticut Avenue, N.W. (downtown); 466-6500. Daytime and evening wear, sportswear, and accessories mainly by American designers.

**Encore of Washington** 3715 Macomb Street, N.W. (uptown); 966-8122. Resale of top American and European labels.

**The Forgotten Woman** Mazza Gallerie, 5300 Wisconsin Avenue, N.W.; 363-0828. Designer fashions in large sizes only.

**Frankie Welch** Of the Capital, Liberty Plaza, 1702 G Street, N.W. (downtown); 466-8900. Daytime and evening wear, accessories and Frankie Welch scarves, of course.

**Gucci Washington** Watergate Mall, 600 New Hampshire Avenue, N.W. (Foggy Bottom); 965-1700. Leather goods and accessories, shoes, scarves, gifts, etc.

**Jameson & Hawkins** 2910 M Street, N.W. (Georgetown); 965-6911. Collection of select vintage Victorian dresses and antique jewelry. Also one-of-a-kind formal evening wear made by Washington designers.

**Laura Ashley** 3213 M Street, N.W. (Georgetown); 338-5481. Fashions for women, teenagers, children, and infants, including dresses, nightgowns, bridal gowns, and clothing accessories in a variety of romantic, Victorian, small country prints, nostalgic designs of the '20s, '30s, '40s and '50s, as well as suave, sophisticated, and elegant patterns.

**Leather Forecast** 218 7th Street, S.E. (Capitol Hill); 547-7337. Shoes, clothing, jewelry, hats, handbags, etc.

**Marie Claire** 1330 Connecticut Avenue (downtown); 466-2680. Also at 1313 Connecticut Avenue, N.W. (downtown); 466-6654. Very good quality French import dresses and accessories.

**Pamela Barkley Boutique** 220 7th Street, S.E. (Capitol Hill); 543-1188. Traditional classic clothing and accessories.

**Saint Laurent Rive Gauche** Watergate Mall, 600 New Hampshire Avenue, N.W. (Foggy Bottom); 965-3555. Daytime and evening wear, sportswear, and accessories.

**The Talbots** 1225 Connecticut Avenue, N.W.; 887-6973. Also in Spring Valley at 4801 Massachusetts Avenue, N.W.; 966-2205. Purely classical clothing for women.

**T. H. Mandy & Co.** 1118 19th Street, N.W. (Dupont Circle); 659-0024. Women's sportswear at discount prices.

**Valentino Boutique** Watergate Mall, 600 New Hampshire Avenue, N.W. (Foggy Bottom); 333-8700. Top designer women's apparel and a few accessories.

**Mothers Work, Washington** 1722 I Street, N.W., in the International Enterprise Bank Building (near Farragut Square Metro stop); 833-1616. Maternity business suits and dresses conservatively styled.

See also SPECIALTY AND GIFT SHOPS; HABERDASHERIES AND TAILORS.

# ZOOS

**National Zoological Park** 3001 Connecticut Avenue, N.W.; 673-4800. Of the more than 2,000 animals, the stars are the giant pandas; they are most active at feeding times, 9 AM and 3 PM. The gibbons are in a large outdoor enclosure that simulates their native habitat. There are also touch-and-discover zoo and bird labs, a herpe lab, white tigers, and a giant aviary. Grounds are open daily, 8 AM–8 PM. Buildings are open daily, 10 AM–5:30 PM and in the summer 'til 6 PM. Parking is extremely limited, with spaces usually filled by 10:30; there is a charge of $3/car. Parking for the handicapped near the Elephant House and lower duck pond. No pets, bicycles, or skateboards allowed in the park. Free admission. Fast-food kiosks and restaurant. Guided tours available by appointment; 673-4955. Inquire about times and locations of animal-training demonstrations. Friends of the National Zoo (FONZ), 673-4960. Woodley Park-Zoo Metro stop.

# MAPS

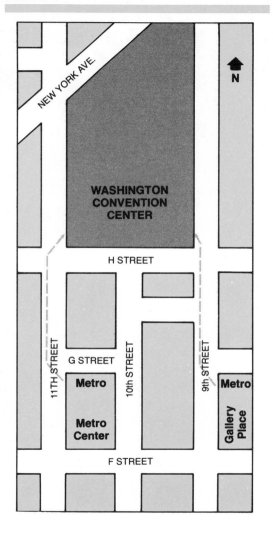

GEORGETOWN

Dumbarton Oaks Park

Dumbarton Oaks

LOVERS LANE

R ST.

RESERVOIR RD.

WISCONSIN AVE

Georgetown University

DENT PL.

Q ST.

VOLTA PL.

34TH ST.

P ST.

31ST ST.

O ST.

O ST.

33RD ST.

POTOMAC ST.

N ST.

PROSPECT ST.

WISCONSIN AVE.

31ST ST.

M ST.

Old Public Market

Chesapeake & Ohio Canal

WHITEHURST FRWY.

WHITEHURST FR

Potomac R.

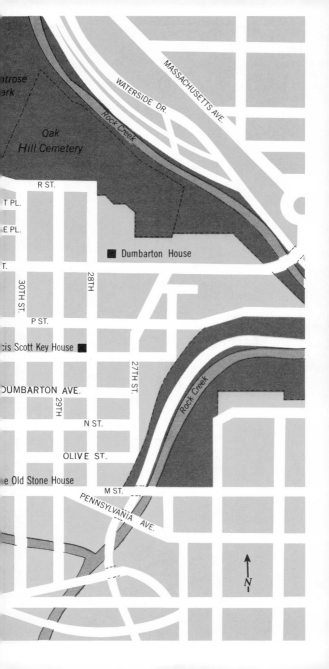

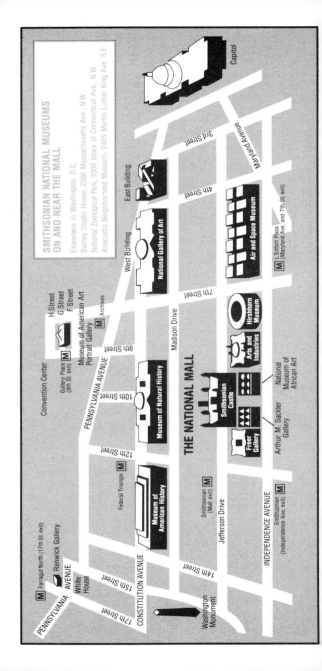

**SMITHSONIAN NATIONAL MUSEUMS ON AND NEAR THE MALL**

Elsewhere in Washington, D.C.
Barney Studio House, 2306 Massachusetts Ave., N.W.
National Zoological Park, 3000 block of Connecticut Ave. N.W.
Anacostia Neighborhood Museum, 2405 Martin Luther King Ave. S.E.

Capitol

East Building

West Building

National Gallery of Art

Air and Space Museum

Ⓜ L'Enfant Plaza (Maryland Ave. and 7th St. exit)

Maryland Avenue

3rd Street

4th Street

7th Street

Hirshhorn Museum

Arts and Industries

National Museum of African Art

Smithsonian Castle

Arthur M. Sackler Gallery

Freer Gallery

**THE NATIONAL MALL**

Madison Drive

Jefferson Drive

INDEPENDENCE AVENUE

Ⓜ Smithsonian (Mall exit)

Ⓜ Smithsonian (Independence Ave. exit)

Museum of Natural History

9th Street

10th Street

12th Street

Convention Center

H Street
G Street
F Street

Museum of American Art
Portrait Gallery

Ⓜ Gallery Place (9th St. exit)

Ⓜ Archives

PENNSYLVANIA AVENUE

Ⓜ Federal Triangle

Museum of American History

14th Street

15th Street

17th Street

CONSTITUTION AVENUE

PENNSYLVANIA AVENUE

Ⓜ Farragut North (17th St. exit)

Renwick Gallery

White House

Washington Monument

# CITIES IN YOUR POCKET

Barron's offers 12 fact-filled *Cities In Your Pocket* guidebooks for just $3.95 each: Atlanta (2534-2), Boston (3767-7), Chicago (3768-5), Hong Kong (3770-7), London (3760-X), Los Angeles (3759-6), New York (3755-3), Paris (3756-1), San Francisco (3758-8), Tokyo (3774-X), Toronto (2836-8), and Washington, D.C. (3757-X). They're in bookstores—or order direct at address below.

# LEARN A LANGUAGE

Barron's leading travelers' language aids will make your trips more satisfying. All are available in bookstores — or order direct from Barron's Educational Series, Inc., 113 Crossways Park Dr., Woodbury, NY 11797, and list title and number. Add 10% ($1.50 minimum) for postage and handling.

## French

**Talking Business In French** Translates 3,000 terms used in business and technology. (3745-6) $6.95
**Now You're Talking French In No Time** A 90-minute cassette of spoken French, 48-page audioscript and *French At A Glance* phrasebook. (7397-5) $9.95
**Getting By In French** A mini-course on two 60-min. cassettes with companion book. (7105-0) $16.95
**Mastering French: Foreign Service Language Inst. Language Series** Develops your fluency: twelve 90-min. cassettes with book. (7321-5) $75.00

## German

**Talking Business In German** Translates 3,000 terms used in business and technology. (3747-2) $6.95

**Now You're Talking German In No Time** A 90-minute cassette of spoken German, 48-page audioscript and *German At A Glance* phrasebook. (7398-3) $9.95

**Getting By In German** A mini-course on two 60-min. cassettes with companion book. (7104-2) $16.95

**Mastering German: Foreign Service Language Inst. Language Series** Develops your fluency: twelve 90-min. cassettes with book. (7352-5) $75.00

## Italian

**Talking Business In Italian** Translates 3,000 terms used in business and technology. (3754-5) $6.95

**Now You're Talking Italian In No Time** A 90-min. cassette of spoken Italian, 48-pg. audioscript and *Italian At A Glance* phrasebook. (7399-1) $9.95

**Getting By In Italian** Mini-course on two 60-min. cassettes with companion book. (7106-9) $16.95

**Mastering Italian: Foreign Service Language Inst. Language Series** Develops your fluency: twelve 90-min. cassettes with book. (7323-1) $75.00

## Japanese

**Now You're Talking Japanese In No Time** 90-min. cassette of spoken Japanese, audioscript and *Japanese At A Glance* phrasebook. (7401-7) $9.95

**Getting By In Japanese** Mini-course on two 60-min. cassettes with companion book. (7150-6) $16.95

## Spanish

**Talking Business In Spanish** Translates 3,000 terms used in business and technology. (3769-3) $6.95

**Now You're Talking Spanish In No Time** A 90-min. cassette of spoken Spanish, 48-page audioscript and *Spanish At A Glance* phrasebook. (7400-9) $9.95

**Getting By In Spanish** A mini-course on two 60-min. cassettes with companion book. (7103-4) $16.95

**Mastering Spanish: Foreign Service Language Inst. Language Series** Develops your fluency: twelve 90-min. cassettes with book. (7325-8) $75.00